Social Studies Made Simple

Grade 3

Written by Kaye Furlong

FS-23223 Social Studies Made Simple Grade 3
All rights reserved—Printed in the U.S.A.
Copyright © 1997 Frank Schaffer Publications
23740 Hawthorne Blvd.
Torrance, CA 90505

Introduction

For young children, whose experience with the world at large is very limited, each new experience sparks interest and curiosity. They want to know how other people live and questions abound.

What was America like before Columbus came?

How can I be a good citizen?

Where did my ancestors come from?

What do people in other countries eat?

Frank Schaffer's Grade 3 *Social Studies Made Simple* provides a wide variety of interesting and challenging activities, projects, and suggestions that are linked to language arts, science, mathematics, and the creative arts. The parts that make up this book are designed and organized to enhance and expand your social studies program. They help students develop thinking and decision-making skills, increase their knowledge and understanding, and become caring, knowledgeable, literate citizens in the local community, state, nation, and the world.

Frank Schaffer's Grade 3 *Social Studies Made Simple* is made up of several sections—geography, culture, history, economics, and government and citizenship. Each section comes with reproducible pages for students to use with specific activities, projects, and ideas.

Social studies encourages students to think about the physical features, natural resources, and climate in America; the history of Native Americans and settlers in relation to the land and its resources; and peoples' ways of life, values, and beliefs. Frank Schaffer's Grade 3 *Social Studies Made Simple* will spark the interests and stimulate the imaginations of your students.

Social Studies

Children are naturally curious about the world they live in—its geography, cultures, history, economy, and values and beliefs. As students learn about these things, they develop an understanding of their roles as citizens and an appreciation of their country's place in the global community.

CONCEPTS

- The bodies of water, the landforms, and the climate of a place affect plant and animal life and people.
- All peoples have the responsibility to conserve earth's resources.
- Availability of water and good soil and a moderate climate affect the development of cities and how people live and work there.
- The cultures of peoples are reflected in their ways of life—including their homes, foods, art forms, and beliefs and values.
- The development of the United States was greatly affected by its natural resources and by the ideals of peoples in its history.
- Our lives are affected by our nation's resources, our work, and trade with other nations.
- We all have responsibilities to participate in our nation's political systems and government.

RESOURCES

Books

Anderson, Joan. *The First Thanksgiving Feast.* Clarion Books, 1984.

Bulla, Clyde R. *Squanto, Friend of the Pilgrims.* Scholastic, 1982.

Cohen, Caron Lee. *The Mud Pony.* Scholastic, 1988.

dePaola, Tomie. *The Legend of the Indian Paintbrush.* Putnam, 1988.

Freedman, Russell. *Buffalo Hunt.* Holiday House, 1988.

George, Jean. *One Day in the Prairie.* Crowel, 1986.

Goble, Paul. *The Girl Who Loved Wild Horses.* Morrow, 1978.

Hoyt-Goldsmith. *Totem Pole.* Holiday House, 1990.

Jeffers, Susan (Illustrator). *Brother Eagle, Sister Sky.* Dial, 1991.

Liptak, Karen. *North American Indian Sign Language.* Franklin Watts, 1982.

Locker, Thomas. *Sky Tree.* HarperCollins, 1995.

Purdy, S. and C. Sandek. *North American Indians.* Franklin Watts, 1982.

Raphael, E. and Bolognese, D. *Sacajawea, The Journey West.* Scholastic, 1994.

Sohi, Morteza. *Look What I Did With a Leaf.* Walker Publishing, 1993.

Winter Jeanette. *Follow the Drinking Gourd.* Alfred A. Knopf, 1988.

Calendars and Art

Fitzpatrick, Shannon. *Native Americans.* (Art Prints). Creative Teaching Press, 1994.

*Wyland calendars, paintings, sculpture. Wyland Studios, 2171 Laguna Canyon Rd. Laguna Beach, CA 92651.

Filmstrips

A Look at Native Americans and *People Behind Our Holidays.* National Geographic Society, Washington, DC 20036.

Geography

Bodies of water, landforms, and climate have profound effects on plants and animals and on the ways people live. The elevation and the availability of water help determine what renewable resources are found on the land and where and how people live on it.

CREATING A MINI-BOOK OF GEOGRAPHY TERMS

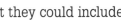

Class Activity

Before students begin the study of bodies of water, provide copies to each student of the two-page *Mini-Book of Geography Terms* on reproducible page 10. Have students cut along the dotted line and glue the two pages back to back. When the bond is dry, have them fold the pages along the center line, making them into a small booklet with the title and the student's name on the first page.

Have students glue or staple extra blank or lined pages inside the cover as needed for additional landforms or physical features. Explain that you will occasionally sketch a physical feature on the board or overhead for students to copy and color into their mini-books. Students can make their cover from a $5'' \times 7\frac{1}{2}''$ sheet of paper so the booklet will be more durable.

KEEPING A SOCIAL STUDIES JOURNAL

Class Activity

Ask your students to keep a journal. Ask students to suggest the types of things that they could include, such as their reactions, thoughts, and ideas about various subjects covered; information learned from current events; and interesting newspaper clippings.

GIVING CURRENT EVENTS REPORTS

Class Activity

Explain that each week, four (or more or fewer) students are to present current events reports and that you will allow time for discussion of the event and report. Tell students to practice giving the report ahead of report time. Point out why it is important to look at the audience frequently. The student should be able to point out the area in which the event took place, and perhaps as the year progresses, begin to relate the event to other events they know about from that area.

Model presenting a current events report. Fill out a copy of student reproducible page 11 and post it with your newspaper clipping on a bulletin board or special corner of the room. Divide the board into Local, National, and World News and put your article and report under the correct heading.

THE EARTH'S BODIES OF WATER

Start a KWL (What We Know, Want to Know, What We Learned) chart. Ask students to name the types of bodies of water with which they are familiar and define them. List their names and definitions in the "Know" section. List the names students have heard but cannot define under "What We Want to Learn." Have students write definitions and draw pictures of the bodies of water as they study them. Place them on the bulletin board as a "What We Learned" display. Remind students to enter definitions of terms into their *Mini-Book of Geography Terms*.

OCEANS, OUR LARGEST BODIES OF WATER

Explain that from earliest times in history people have lived near oceans because they provided food and because traveling and transporting goods on water was easier than doing so over land. Locate the major oceans on a large physical world map. Discuss why water is generally shown in blue on maps. Provide a copy of the map on reproducible page 12 to each student. Ask the class to label the oceans and the continents, using reference materials to find names and locations.

WATER WEIGHT

Help students understand that water is one of nature's most powerful forces. Make or buy a pinwheel. Place the pinwheel under gently running water and point out that even a tiny stream of water has enough power to turn the wheel. Then allow students to get a feel for the weight of water by filling a large bucket with water and have students sit or stoop to try to move it. (Make sure they do not lift or carry it!)

Have the class use sand and mud to create mountain shapes in a baking pan or plastic container. Ask students to create a flow of water running down their mountains by pouring water from a pitcher. As more and more of the water flows down the mountains, the grooves should deepen and some of the "mountains" should be carried to the bottom of the pan showing how water carves and moves land.

Brainstorm to make a list of facts that students already know about oceans. Then provide each student with a copy of "Amazing Oceans" on reproducible page 13. Instruct the class to read the page and complete the activities. Afterward, discuss how land is shaped by oceans.

RESOURCES OF THE OCEAN

Organize students into teams to make an ocean mural with plants, animals, and a surface section showing fishing boats and ships to indicate ways people use the ocean. To make the art vivid, have them use oil pastels or colored chalk on damp paper.

OCEAN ANIMALS WITH SHELLS

Display any seashells you may have collected and bring books on seashells to class. Encourage students to share collections they may have. Provide time for students to examine the shells and books. Then have class members tell what they already know about the kinds of animals that lived in the shells. Brainstorm a list of questions on animals living in seashells: Where do they live? What do they eat? How do they make the shells? What happens when a shell becomes too small for an animal? Encourage students to read the books in class and check other sources to find answers to their questions.

WHERE AND HOW OCEAN MAMMALS LIVE

Form small groups to do a research report on mammals that live in the ocean, such as whales, dolphins, sea lions, and so on. Suggest that each group find out what the mammals eat, where they live, whether they live together or alone, and whether other animals eat them as food. Encourage students to make a sketch of their mammals or to find pictures in books to bring to class. Have each group present its report orally.

RIVERS, LAKES, AND OTHER BODIES OF WATER

Display a large wall map of the United States and provide a copy of "Important Rivers and Lakes in the United States" on reproducible page 14 to each student. Ask students to use the wall map or maps in their textbooks to complete the activity.

Help students visualize the movement of water in rivers and streams. Using a cookie sheet, allow water to drip onto an almost flat surface. Gradually tip the cookie sheet more and more to create a greater angle. Challenge students to explain why water moves much faster when it is running down a steep path from a mountain than when it meanders across almost flat land. Provide a copy of reproducible page 15, "Understanding Rivers and Lakes" to each student. Instruct the class to read it and complete the activity. Discuss the attributes and effects of rivers and other bodies of water. Lead students to understand that possibly the most impressive thing about a river is its ability to carve away land, or deposit new land.

Encourage students to learn more about the Grand Canyon. Invite them to bring to class a variety of pictures of the canyon for everyone to enjoy. Display a large map of the United States. Invite students to locate the Mississippi and Colorado rivers and trace the course of each, beginning at the source and ending at the mouth. Challenge students to explain to the class how and why the erosion of the land of the two rivers would be different.

FS-23223 Social Studies Made Simple ■ © Frank Schaffer Publications, Inc.

STUDYING LOCAL BODIES OF WATER ······ Class Activity ·····

If a body of water is located in your area, visit it with students, if possible. Ask them to draw pictures about their experiences there. If a visit is not possible, ask students to research and write about the body of water. Allow time for presentation of students' findings and written work.

USING "WATER WORDS" IN POEMS ······ Class Activity ·····

Brainstorm to create a list of "water words," including words about oceans, rivers, lakes, streams, and so on. Encourage students to close their eyes and think of words that tell what they hear, smell, feel or touch, as well as see. Categorize the words under headings naming the bodies of water. Model writing a poem using the words under one of the headings. Have students use any of the words they wish to create a short poem about water. Remind them that poems need not rhyme.

WHAT ARE THE DIFFERENT LANDFORMS AND LAND REGIONS? ······ Class Activity ·····

Explain to the class that a traveler crossing the United States would see many kinds of landforms: mountains, cliffs, canyons, plateaus, craters, swamps, dunes, plains. The name a landform is given depends mostly on elevation. Elevation is the distance above or below sea level. Hills are lower than mountains, and plains are flat or gently rolling areas. Discuss what students already know about prairie, desert, forest, and mountain areas. Invite them to share pictures and recollections of visits to such areas. Provide a copy of reproducible page 16, "Things to See in the Mountains and Deserts," to students and ask them to complete the activity. Invite students to share their pictures with the class.

READING ABOUT THE LAND ······ Class Activity ·····

Obtain books about different landforms and land regions and the animals that live in them. Have students help to arrange them around the classroom. Add magazines such as *National Geographic* and *Ranger Rick* to the collection. Calendars with pictures of mountains, deserts, and so on would also be useful. Materials produced by the Sierra Club and Audubon Society will fit students' studies of geographical areas and the plant and animal life found there. Encourage students to read and use these materials.

WHERE COULD I SEE A CRATER? ······ Group Activity ·····

Form small groups. Have each group find information on one landform, such as a crater or a plateau, and to draw a picture of it. Encourage the groups to write a definition, a short description, and a location for their landform. Have each group share its findings. Encourage the class to add definitions to their *Mini-Book of Geographic Terms.*

MOUNTAINS AND PLAINS

Display a large map of the United States. Invite students to indicate the plains and mountainous areas, using the map key and what they know about elevation. Have students locate the mountain range closest to your area. Help them use the map key to check the heights of mountains in the range.

Explain that about one-fifth of the earth's surface is covered by mountains 2,000 feet or more above sea level. Some mountains form when the earth's crust folds, when the crust breaks into giant blocks, or when it rises to form a dome. Other mountains form when volcanoes erupt again and again, spewing out lava or ash that form layers. Ask students to speculate why a plains area, which is flat or has low hills, could become a mountainous area. Provide a copy of reproducible page 20 on prairies and have students complete it. After completion, discuss the importance of prairies as well as the students' outlines.

RELIEF MAPS OF MOUNTAINS AND PLAINS

Enlarge and copy the United States map on reproducible page 14, making two copies for each student. Enlarge the maps on the copier. Using one map, have students cut out the continental United States and glue it onto a large piece of cardboard. Provide a large physical map as a guide and ask students to draw in these mountain ranges on the map: Coastal, Cascade, Sierra Nevada, Rocky Mountains, and Appalachian. On the second copy of the map, have them indicate and label the Central Valley, the Great Basin, the Great and Central Plains, and the Gulf and Atlantic Coastal Plains. Tell students they will use this map as a guide while they work with dough. Provide a container, a plastic bag, and a copy of the following recipe for each student:

DOUGH RECIPE ·······························

- *Mix 2 cups flour and 2 cups salt.*
- *Add water to the mixture and knead it until it is similar to clay. If it becomes too stiff add a little water. If it is too moist, add flour.*
- *Save the dough in a plastic bag and seal the bag.*

Model how to make the relief map. Put a layer of dough on the map on the cardboard. Pinch up the mountains, form valleys, and flatten areas to indicate plains. Make the Rockies and the tips of the Sierra Nevadas a bit higher than the other mountain ranges. Ask students to make their own relief maps and to paint them using tempera paints. Have students label the mountain ranges, valleys, and plains and make a map key.

HOW ARE ROCKS FORMED?

Class Activity

Invite students who have rock collections to bring them to class. If you have a rock collection of your own, display it and invite the class to examine the rocks to see how they differ from one another. Organize students into groups and have each group find out how one kind of rock is formed. Arrange for each group to share its findings.

WEATHER AND CLIMATE IN MOUNTAINS AND DESERTS

Class Activity

Point out that weather is probably one of the most important characteristics of deserts and mountains. Discuss why few people live on high mountains (cold weather, difficult getting roads put in, erecting buildings, utilities, etc.) and in hot, dry deserts. Invite students to draw an outfit for visiting a snow-covered mountain and one for visiting the desert during the summer.

Discuss the effects of sunlight, both to our advantage and disadvantage, and the importance of wearing sunscreen. Plants and people use the sunlight, but overexposure can cause future problems. Ask students what they know about the importance of wearing sunscreen products and sunglasses to avoid physical problems.

Explain that mountains have a strong effect on weather and climate. As clouds move from west to east, they rise to pass over the mountains. Since the air is cooler at higher elevations, they cannot hold the water as well, so it is dropped as rain or snow on the western side of the mountains. The eastern side receives much less rain or snow, so fewer plants can grow there.

ANIMALS OF THE MOUNTAINS

Class Activity

Explain that mountains have animal inhabitants that have adapted to their environments in special ways. Lower areas of mountains may have forests, where forest animals live. At the top of mountains where it is very cold, bighorn animals may stay only part of the year, coming down to lower elevations to find food during colder months. Animals such as mountain lions may hunt their prey, such as deer and elk, mainly at night. They may also eat skunks and porcupines when larger animals are not available. These animals may be helpful since they will eat old and diseased deer. Discuss the ways in which the animals have adapted. Then ask students to create posters showing animals of the mountains.

THE DESERT AND ITS ANIMALS AND PLANTS

Tell students that much of the earth's surface is desert. A desert is a region that gets little rain or snow. Desert land can be rocky or sandy and the soil is often poor. Few plants and animals live in desert areas where there is little precipitation. In deserts that receive more moisture, many kinds of plants and animals have adapted to desert living and are able to thrive. Discuss how animals get their water in an area where little rain falls and rivers and lakes are not nearby (from food such as seeds, plants, the bodies of other animals they eat, and so on).

Students may wish to bring to class or make personal sketch books to draw desert flowers, trees, and animals. Introduce them to using the sides of their pencils for shading. They can keep the book throughout the year and take it home for vacation practice.

EXPERIMENTING WITH SOILS AND PLANTS

Set out two small glass jars of soil, one with sandy, rocky soil and one with rich soil (planter mix). Pour a little water into each jar so students can observe that the water seeps right through the sandy soil but is absorbed by the rich soil. Explain that desert plants must "drink" and store as much water as possible when there is rain so they can use it when there is none. Cut open a small cactus to show how the plant stores water.

Plant two types of plants in good soil as well as in sandy soil. Water the plants in the good soil often and those in sandy soil less often. Have students observe the plants for a few weeks. Then help them conclude that plants growing in areas with much rainfall and good soil need different conditions than those growing in sandy soil or where there is little rainfall. Challenge students to hypothesize why cactuses have thorns.

Art Project

Making a **M**ountain and **D**esert **M**ural

Plan a mountain and desert mural with the class. The mural could show mountain areas in the middle, with clouds dropping rain on the west where lots of trees are growing. On the east, the mural could have a desert with a variety of cactus plants, especially the Saguaro, and desert animal life. Students could include a "The Desert Comes Alive at Night" section. Make the mural a group project and share the mural with other classes. To extend the activity, have students complete the activity on reproducible page 19.

ENJOYING LITERATURE

Class Activity

Obtain a copy of *Sam, Bangs, and Moonshine* and read it aloud to the class. Afterward, discuss the difference between imagination for story writing and the harm that almost came from carrying it beyond that point. Suggest students pretend to be Sam and write letters to her friend apologizing for her behavior and so on.

HOW PEOPLE USE FORESTS

Class Activity

Explain to students that before settlers from Europe began clearing the land, forests covered most of America. Now they cover about one-third of the land in the continental United States. Invite students to name as many products made from wood as they can and list them on the chalkboard. Discuss the reasons for the decline in forest lands (include land for farming and building towns and cities), why we need to protect our forests, and what people can do to save forests.

Art Project

The Forest and Its Animals

Invite students to make a group mural illustrating how various kinds of animals are dependent on the forests and how the animals help the forest survive. They could draw animals such as squirrels, birds, raccoons, and insects, showing how they make their homes in the branches, trunks, or bark of trees. They could also show what the animals eat—seeds, nuts, bark, leaves, wood, and roots. Remind students to include predators (animals that hunt other animals for food).

Point out that the forest is also dependent on animals. Birds that eat berries and seeds scatter some to the ground, some of which grow into berry plants or trees. Squirrels and mice bury nuts in the ground, and those they do not eat may grow into trees. When animals die, their bodies decay and make the soil richer.

HOW TREES GROW

Class Activity

Challenge students to find a tree that was cut down or fell down. Ask them to measure the tree around the trunk using a tape measure and draw a cross section of the tree showing growth rings. Have students guess the approximate age of the tree. Explain that when a tree is cut, it shows rings of growth. In years with plenty of rainfall, the rings will be wide. In years of drought (little rainfall), the rings will be narrow. Trees add about one inch to their girth each year, so a tree that is twelve inches around, is about twelve years old.

Extend the activity by having students complete a report on forest or prairie animals on reproducible page 21.

WHY LEAVES CHANGE COLOR

Invite students to bring to class a variety of leaves found in your area (if possible, fall leaves of different colors). Discuss why leaves change colors (when trees are ready to shed leaves, the supply of water is cut off and the chlorophyll, which gives the green color, breaks down, allowing the other colors to show). Assign students to work with a partner to identify their leaves using encyclopedias or other sources. Pass out reproducible page 17, "Learning More About Forests" to extend the activity.

Art Project

Enjoying Trees and the Four Seasons

Provide each student four 9" × 12" sheets to create four season calendars showing a tree during each of the seasons. Also provide old toothbrushes and tempera paints, including white to represent snow. After students complete their pictures, cut up a large calendar into the four seasons and provide a set of photocopies of it to each student. Help students mount their drawings or paintings on separate sheets of paper with the calendars for each season below them. Then punch and tie the four sheets together.

LEARNING MORE ABOUT PRAIRIES

Provide a copy of reproducible page 20 on prairies and have students complete it. After completion, discuss the importance of prairies as well as the students' outlines.

CELEBRATING OUR COUNTRY IN SONGS

Sing such songs with students as "The Erie Canal" to help them relate the importance of waterways to the lives of people in the past. The songs, "America" and "This Land Is Your Land," tell of such places as forests, mountains, "waves of grain," "plains," "sea to shining sea," "gulf stream waters," "golden valley," and "diamond deserts." Sing them with the class to add variety to the study of social studies. Discuss how these songs foster pride in America and why they are an important part of the American culture.

Extend the activity by having students look at where people live in the different U.S. geographic regions. Pass out copies of reproducible page 22 and have students complete the activity.

A GEOGRAPHIC CONCLUSION

To conclude the geography unit and provide a bridge to the unit on culture, have students complete reproducible page 23, "Fun With Poetry."

plain: a broad flat area of land	**My Mini-Book of Geography Terms** by _____
prairie: a large level area of grassland	**bay:** part of a lake or ocean extending into the land
river: a large stream of water that flows into another body of water such as an ocean or lake	**canyon:** a narrow valley with high, steep, sides
valley: low land between hills or mountains	**coast:** the land next to an ocean

✂ -

desert: a dry area where few plants grow	**island:** a body of land surrounded by water
forest: an area of land where many trees grow	**lake:** a body of water surrounded by land
harbor: a protected body of water forming a safe shelter where ships can stop	**mountain:** a steeply raised mass of land
hill: a raised mass of land, not as large as a mountain	**ocean:** a body of salt water covering a large part of the earth

Current Events Report

1. Choose an article that will make an interesting report.

2. Make sure you understand the main ideas.

3. Look up words you do not know in a dictionary.

4. Answer the questions below.

5. Attach it to your report.

Title or headline of article _____

Where the article came from _____

What the article is about _____

What happened? _____

_____

When did it happen? _____

Where did it happen? _____

How did it happen? _____

_____

Name _____

Oceans and Continents

Label all the oceans and continents. Then use a blue colored pencil to shade in the oceans.

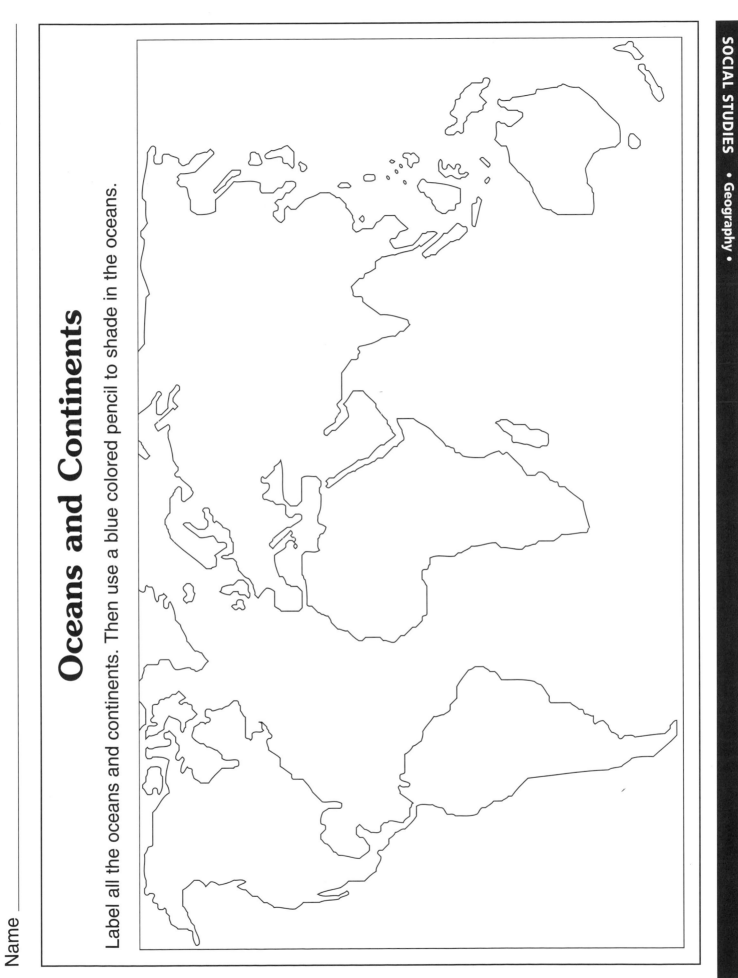

Name _____

The Amazing Oceans

About seventy percent of the earth's surface is covered by five oceans. Five salty oceans surround the world's seven continents. Oceans change the shape of the shoreline a little bit each day.

Sometimes waves wash up on a shore and leave sand and mud behind. In other places, powerful ocean waves carve away rock. They crush shells and rock into sand and carry the sand away. The process is called erosion. The force of the waves forms cliffs along some parts of the coast, the land at the edge of the ocean.

People use the oceans to get fish and shellfish and to transport goods and people. People also use the oceans for fun. They boat, swim, surf, and fish in the ocean and relax on the beach.

Answer the questions below. Write complete sentences.

1. How do oceans change the land? _____

_____

_____

_____

_____

2. In what important ways do people use the oceans? _____

_____

_____

_____

_____

Try This!   On a blank sheet of paper, draw a picture showing what you would do at the beach.

FS-23223 Social Studies Made Simple ▪ © Frank Schaffer Publications, Inc.

Important Rivers and Lakes in the United States

Label these rivers on a map of the United States: Mississippi and Missouri. Next label these lakes and color them blue: Michigan, Superior, Huron, Erie, and Ontario. Also label the Pacific and Atlantic oceans.

Understanding Rivers and Lakes

Rivers are freshwater streams of flowing water. Rivers start from a source, such as a spring, an underground stream, or melting snow in the mountains. Many people use river water for drinking after it is treated to make it pure. Many animals live in or near rivers.

When rivers flood, they may leave stone, gravel, and sand beyond their banks. Like oceans, they can wear away soil and rocks, and even carve out canyons. The Colorado River carved the famous Grand Canyon over millions of years. Large rivers like the Mississippi are important for transporting goods.

Lakes are large pools of fresh water. Large lakes like Lake Michigan are also used to transport goods. Lakes also provide homes for water animals, food for people, and places for recreation.

Use the information on this page and what you learned about oceans to fill in the chart below.

	Kind of Water	Movement	Uses	Effect on Land
Rivers				
Lakes				
Oceans				

FS-23223 Social Studies Made Simple ■ © Frank Schaffer Publications, Inc.

Things to See in the Mountains and Deserts

Draw things you could do and see in the mountains and in the desert.

Mountain Area	Desert Area

Learning More About Forests

In forests, tree roots help prevent erosion because they soak up water and grasp the soil so the wind cannot blow it away. The trees' leaves take in carbon dioxide and give off oxygen so that people and animals have clean air to breathe. When trees die, they decay, making the soil richer.

Forests provide food and homes for wildlife. Birds and squirrels live in tree branches. Insects live in tree bark, and raccoons and birds often live in holes in tree trunks. Nuts, seeds, bark, leaves, wood, and roots provide food for the animals.

Animals also help the forests. Some animals scatter seeds or bury nuts which may grow into new trees. When the animals die, their bodies decay and make the soil richer so the trees grow better. We can say that trees and animals depend on each other.

Writing a Summary

Write the main idea from the story above. Then write a summary in your own words about what you just read.

Main Idea: _____

_____

_____

Summary: _____

_____

_____

_____

_____

_____

_____

FS-23223 Social Studies Made Simple • © Frank Schaffer Publications, Inc.

How Animals and Plants Survive in the Desert

Living in a hot, dry desert is hard for plants and animals. They have to adapt to survive. Some plants grow long roots to absorb moisture from deep in the soil. Others store water in stems and leaves for dry periods. Cactus plants have thorns to keep thirsty animals from eating them to get moisture. Some desert animals burrow underground and come out only in the early morning or at night, when it is cooler, to look for food. Some animals, such as iguanas, rest in the shade of rocks or plants when it is hot and cover themselves with sand if they are cool. Desert animals get water by eating plants, seeds, or other animals.

Plants and animals living in colder deserts adapt differently. The Gila monster stores fat in its tail. When food is scarce, the Gila monster's body uses the stored fat.

Categorizing Information

Below list the facts about how animals or plants survive in the desert. Add any ideas you learned from your textbook, other books, or magazines.

PLANTS	ANIMALS

Spotlight On: The Saguaro Cactus

Saguaro cactuses can grow 50 feet tall and live for 250 years. They do not start growing arms until they are about 75 years old. To save water, the saguaro's beautiful blossoms close before the sun becomes hot during the day. Its huge trunk can store hundreds of gallons of water, and its roots go deep to soak up rainwater. Arizona's Native Americans have used saguaro stems for fuel and building houses and the fruit for food.

Animals, too, use the saguaros. You might even call them desert animal hotels. Owls, woodpeckers, and other birds make homes inside saguaros. Doves or hawks build nests in saguaro arms. Coyotes eat fallen saguaro fruit and jack rabbits nibble saguaro sprouts. Wood rats, shrews, kangaroo rats, and snakes nest beneath the saguaro roots.

Finding Facts

List five or more interesting facts about the saguaro cactus.

1. _____

_____

2. _____

_____

3. _____

_____

4. _____

_____

5. _____

_____

Try This!

Find a picture of the saguaro in an encyclopedia under guideword *cactus,* in your textbook, or in a book on desert plants.

The Prairies

Prairies are large areas of grass-covered flat or rolling land. On their way west, pioneers thought the prairies looked like a sea of waving grass. The prairies extend from Canada to Texas and cover much of Oklahoma, Kansas, Nebraska, Iowa, Illinois, North Dakota, and South Dakota.

Some pioneers decided to stop their journey west when they reached the prairies. They made their first homes from sod (soil held together by grass) because almost no trees grew on the prairies. Then they farmed the rich prairie soil or used the grass to feed cattle on large ranches.

Prairies, like forests, provide homes for animals. Prairie dogs and badgers dig tunnels, or burrows, under the ground. Pronghorn antelope graze on prairie grasses. Coyotes run fast and leap long distances to catch and eat other animals.

Outlining

Outlining helps you organize main ideas and details.

Use the story above to fill in details on the outline.

I. Not all pioneers traveling westward crossed the prairies.

   A. _____

   B. _____

II. Prairies provide homes for animals.

   A. _____

   B. _____

• Geography • SOCIAL STUDIES

Writing a Report on a Forest or Prairie Animal

Find information and write a report on one of the forest or prairie animals below. Name the animal and describe it and its home. Tell what the animal eats, who its enemies are, and how it protects itself. Also tell anything else you find interesting about it.

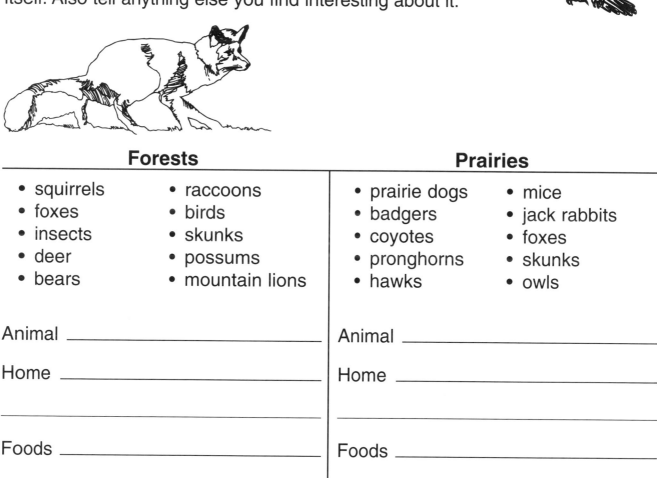

Forests		Prairies	
• squirrels	• raccoons	• prairie dogs	• mice
• foxes	• birds	• badgers	• jack rabbits
• insects	• skunks	• coyotes	• foxes
• deer	• possums	• pronghorns	• skunks
• bears	• mountain lions	• hawks	• owls

Animal _____

Home _____

_____

Foods _____

_____

Enemies _____

_____

_____

How it protects itself _____

_____

_____

Animal _____

Home _____

_____

Foods _____

_____

Enemies _____

_____

_____

How it protects itself _____

_____

_____

Where Do Most People Live?

Most people live in cities. Cities grow in certain locations because the things people want and need are nearby. A location near rivers and oceans means that transportation for goods is available. A location near land where food can be easily grown and where the climate is not too hot or cold, means that people will have enough to eat and jobs growing crops. As more people come, businesses and manufacturers have more workers. More people buy products. More people come to find jobs. Cities also grow in places where recreation is available.

Clustering Ideas

One way to organize ideas is to group them into clusters. Fill in the chart below, including information on why people choose to live in your area. You can call your local Chamber of Commerce or a real estate office for information.

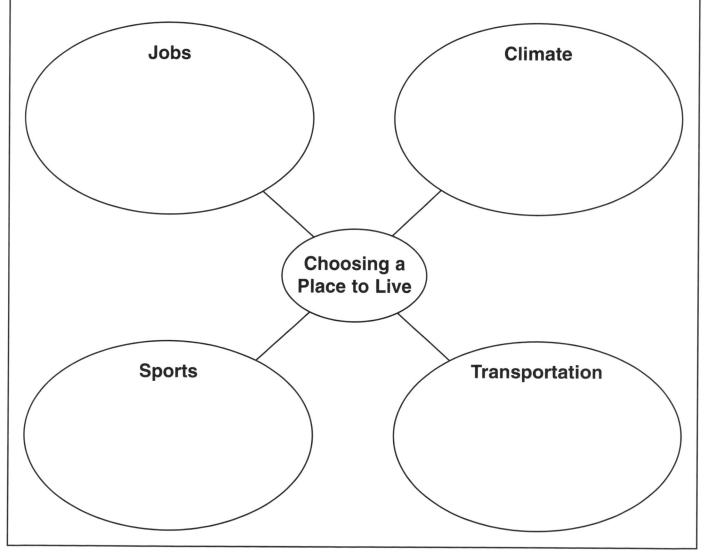

Fun With Poetry

Below each heading, write a list of words that reminds you of what you studied. Use the words to write a poem. You can write about one region or a little about each region.

Forests

Prairies

_____

_____

_____

_____

_____

_____

Mountains

Deserts

_____

_____

_____

_____

_____

_____

FS-23223 Social Studies Made Simple ■ © Frank Schaffer Publications, Inc.

Culture

The Native American groups, or tribes, had a rich and varied culture before the arrival of the European settlers. The way of life of each group—including their homes, foods, arts, and customs and beliefs—was closely related to the natural environment of the region in which they lived.

THE WAYS OF LIFE OF NATIVE AMERICAN TRIBES

Class Activity

Explain that groups of Native Americans lived for thousands of years on the American continent. Over time, these peoples developed their own special ways of life. The homes, clothes, foods, arts, ceremonies, and beliefs of the groups of tribes were greatly affected by the natural resources of the regions in which they lived. Invite students to name what natural resources were available to Native Americans living near bodies of water, in forests, on the prairies, and on the desert.

USING A JOURNAL AND MINI-DICTIONARY

Class Activity

Tell students to begin a journal in which they are to write information and draw sketches on the various Native American groups they will be studying.

Provide several sheets of paper to each student. Ask students to make a mini-dictionary of terms similar to the one they have made for the geography section. Encourage them to enter all new terms with their definitions in their dictionaries as they are learning about Indian tribes.

REPORTS ON NATIVE AMERICAN NATIONS

Class Activity

Provide a copy of reproducible page 33 to each student. Explain to the class that they will be filling out reports on various Native American groups as they study them. Tell students that you will provide additional copies as they need them. (Make a stack of copies and keep them on hand.)

TAKING NOTES

Class Activity

Model notetaking on the board, including writing about material from a text in one's own words. Illustrate how students can use some words from a text without copying the text.

Have students practice notetaking, using a text or material you read aloud. Students can use the outline method or just use words and phrases. Invite individuals to read their notes aloud. Stress the importance of using one's own words.

READING BOOKS AND STORIES

Read a short book of fiction and a non-fiction book aloud and have others available for students to read. Show all illustrations. Explain that reading literature will help students appreciate and empathize with people of other times and places, as well as with people of today. Point out that many Native American stories and legends show the importance of nature to Native Americans. Often, the legends explain natural events such as how rainbows began. Invite students to choose a book of their own to read.

Provide a variety of books or stories for the students to read and tell aloud to the class. You may want to videotape the presentations to use for an open house or other times when you have visitors, or just for children to see and evaluate their work.

NATIVE AMERICANS OF THE NORTHWEST

Explain that the Native American nations of the Northwest, including the Kwakiutl tribe, had similar ways of meeting their needs since they had the same natural resources available. Ask students to name things that the ocean and rivers provide (foods, transportation, recreation, etc.).

Brainstorm a list of foods that Native Americans from this region may have been able to get from the sea (crabs, clams, mussels, seaweed, salmon, cod, herring, halibut). Explain that the Native Americans also used sea lions, otters, seals, and porpoises for food and furs.

Provide reproducible page 34 to students and ask them to complete the page. Afterward, discuss how extra fish and meat from forest animals could be dried for use during the winter when hunting and fishing were more difficult.

WAS IT WRONG TO WEAR FUR?

Organize the class into two groups. Ask one group to give reasons why they think the killing of animals for furs was necessary for the Native Americans' survival. Ask the other group to argue why they think it was not necessary. The class may conclude that the Native Americans needed the furs because they had no suitable substitute for furs. Stress that part of the belief system of Native Americans was that they should take from the land and sea only what they needed. Native Americans were not wasteful.

Ask students to compare the Native Americans' need for fur with today's uses. Discuss why people today stress conservation of wildlife.

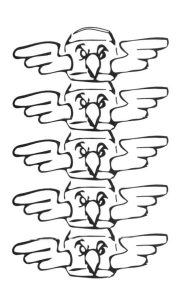

Ways of **G**etting **F**oods

Have students sketch various ways the Native Americans got food from their environment, including seafood and fish. Encourage them to show that some foods could be collected and hunted in the forest, some could be caught in basket types of traps and in nets, and some could be caught with spears, harpoons, rakes, and hooks. Display their drawings on a bulletin board.

USING THE FOREST

Class Activity

Provide copies of reproducible pages 35 and 36 to students and ask them to read and complete the pages.

Ask students to make small drawings showing items made from trees for Native American use, including homes and furniture, giant totem poles, large canoes, babies' diapers, lining for cradles, clothing, mats, and tablecloths. Use these drawings to make a chart. Display it on the bulletin board.

Discuss the ways the availability of trees shaped the arts and crafts of the Native Americans of the northwest. Point out that masks, totems, canoes, and furniture were carved with intricate designs. Discuss the amount of time and talent or skill that carving a totem pole requires. Help students to realize that not everyone could afford to have a totem pole.

NOW AND THEN: COMPARING FOREST USES

Class Activity

Compare how forests provide for us today with how they may have provided for the Native Americans long ago. Begin a chart of the ways we benefit from forest regions. As students continue to study the Native Americans of the Northwest, extend the chart to include the ways they benefited. Have students identify any benefits that are the same for us as they were for Native Americans.

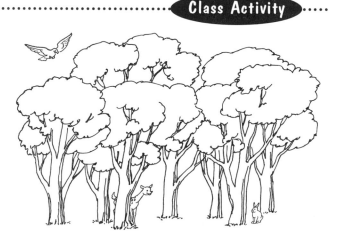

Discuss why there are some differences between our need for forests and Native Americans' need for them several hundred years ago, such as our need for clean air. Also discuss why protecting our forests is important. Be sure students realize that the population of North America has changed drastically, and forests have been cleared to the point that we need to protect what we have.

RESPECT FOR NATURE

Explain that Native Americans protected and respected nature by neither taking too much of anything nor wasting anything. For example, they did not peel off too much bark or the tree might be damaged. Ask students to give examples of how we respect and protect our forests and animals (forbidding or limiting hunting, limiting tree cutting, planting new trees, recycling paper products).

COMPARING LONG HOUSES WITH MODERN HOUSES

Show pictures of long houses and explain that Kawkiutl long houses were up to 60 feet long and were used by three or four families.

Ask students to compare long houses with houses today. Provide sheets of paper and instruct students to fold them in half. On one half, have them draw the Native American homes, food, clothing, and other items such as a totem pole. On the other half, have them show similar objects from their own lives. They could, for example, compare a photo album to a totem pole and show a family gathering or other celebration next to Native Americans in masks, celebrating an event.

Art Project

Totem Poles

Read aloud the story, *Totem Pole,* by Diane Hoyt-Goldsmith, (Holiday House, 1990) telling of a Tsimshian boy and his father who carves totem poles. Discuss the craft of making totem poles and the ceremony involved in raising the totem pole.

Provide a copy of reproducible page 37 to each student and have students create totem poles. For the totem poles, provide 5" × 7" index cards or cut cardstock or tagboard to the same size. Also provide the materials listed on the student page. Ask students to follow the directions on the pages to make the totem poles. Display the completed totem poles with descriptions or reasons for having a totem pole. Encourage students to pretend to be speechmakers and tell about the animals on their totem poles.

Ask the class to create a large group totem pole from tagboard and colored paper or paint. Encourage them to write stories explaining the totem pole. Then have a totem pole raising at which students sing songs and do the toe-heel dance. If time permits, suggest they make costumes to wear at the party.

Art **P**roject

Masks and **C**eremonies

Explain that many carved items, such as masks and rattles, were used in Native American ceremonies. Masks generally showed animals and represented something in life that reminded Native Americans of that animal.

Provide a copy of reproducible page 38 to each student and make the materials listed on the page available to the class for making masks. Cut a large mask shape from tagboard so students can use it for tracing. It should be similar to the one shown, but increased to the desired size. Ask students to cut out their own shape from tagboard or heavy paper. You could have an adult cut out the eye parts.

MAKING COMPARISONS

Class Activity

Ask students to do research on tribes who lived in the Northeastern woodlands to find similarities and differences in the ways Native Americans on opposite coasts lived. Have them study such tribes as the Chippewa, Delaware, Iroquois, or Wampanoag (who helped the Pilgrims). Provide copies of reproducible page 33 and encourage students to follow the format on the page.

Art **P**roject

Making a **D**iorama or **T**able **S**cene

Invite students to make a diorama or a tabletop scene showing the life of the Northwest Native Americans. Provide soil or sand and a cardboard base to which the sand can be glued. Suggest students make trees from twigs and real leaves; hilly areas from clay; and long houses from paper, cloth, mud and grass, or craft sticks. Remind the class that the Northwest Native Americans built their long houses close together, facing the sea.

MAKING A MURAL

Class Activity

Invite students to plan a mural showing how the Northwest Native Americans lived. Ask them to show houses, the people and their use of trees and forests, and the resources of the area. Tell students that they can include art objects and any other items they wish. After the mural is completed, display it and invite visitors to view it. Encourage the students to write and present information about the area or make the presentations on tapes or videotapes to be played for the visitors. Also display any written poems, songs, or stories the students may have written.

NATIVE AMERICANS OF
THE PLAINS: THE CHEYENNE

Explain that in the 1500s, the Cheyenne were hunters and fishers in the Great Lakes area. Gradually they were pushed from that area by the Sioux and the Ojibwa. They moved to the plains area and became farmers. Because the weather was unpredictable, life on the plains was difficult. The Cheyenne hunted buffalo on foot. The women's job on the hunt was carrying or pulling heavy loads. In the 1750s, when the Cheyenne began to hunt on horseback, they followed the buffalo all year long and gave up farming.

Discuss the differences in availability of resources in the prairies and forests. Ask students how the lives of the Native Americans might have changed after they got horses.

Provide a copy of reproducible page 39 to each student. After completion, have the class make a list or drawing of the Native Americans' resource, the buffalo, and the things the buffalo provided to meet the Native Americans' needs.

THE BUFFALO IN THE LIVES OF
PLAINS NATIVE AMERICANS

Read the book, *Buffalo Hunt,* by Russell Freedman to students. Discuss the buffalo hunt from beginning to end, including the drying of hides for making clothing and tipis. Help students understand the need for portable homes for people who depended on the buffalo. Provide a copy of reproducible page 40 to each student. After completion, have students compare the Native Americans' ways of getting clothes with their own way of getting clothes.

NATIVE AMERICAN LIFE

Help students visualize the uses and activities associated with the buffalo. Display the book *Buffalo Hunt* and the Native Americans art study prints (*See* Resources page). Then invite students to sketch or paint some Native American scenes of their own.

WHERE ARE THE BUFFALO?

Ask interested students to research the buffalo, including its size, reproduction rates, origins, and so on. Encourage them to find out why there are so few buffalo today. Pose the question: Will there be many more buffalo in the future if they are protected and encouraged to reproduce?

The Movable Tipi

Provide a copy of reproducible page 41 to each student. Invite students to make miniature tipis and set up a miniature village. Ask students to plan the village as a group.

Invite students to study the art reproductions and make tiny buffalo from construction paper. Ask them to cut pretend hides and put them on the ground with twigs or toothpick pieces for stakes. Point out that they can use twigs to make a frame and stitch thin string through the pretend hides to stretch them on the frame. Suggest that they can add grasses or grass-like plants to a base made from soil or earth.

What Is a Parfleche?

Make a hide shape from tagboard for students to trace around and have large grocery bags on hand. Invite students to make hides. Instruct them to cut the hide from a large grocery sack using the tagboard shape. Have them dampen the hide and crumple it repeatedly until it is soft. When it is dry they can use black or brown markers to draw designs on the hide. Hang the hides in the room. Provide a copy of reproducible page 43 to each student. Encourage students to work in groups. Give advice when asked.

HOW DID THEY DO IT?

Group Activity

Form small groups and have students dramatize events in the Plains Native Americans' lives, such as hunting buffalo, putting up a tipi, preparing the hides, (see reproducible page 42) and so on.

BELIEFS OF THE PLAINS NATIVE AMERICANS

Class Activity

Discuss the importance of nature, especially of rain, in the lives of farmers. Rain is essential for the growth of crops as well as for the growth of grasses. Ask students to tell what they already know about the Native American rain dance. Also discuss the importance of symbols in our lives as well as in the lives of the Plains Native Americans. Ask students to brainstorm a list of some symbols in our country, such as the flag, the eagle, and Liberty Bell. Point out that an important symbol in Cheyenne life was the tree, which was a part of the cycle of nature. Provide a copy of reproducible page 44 to each student. Ask students to complete the page. Afterward, discuss the role of the medicine man and the purpose of the medicine dance.

RELATING TO OUR LIVES
····· Class Activity ·····

Ask students to write or discuss about how their lives would be different if their families had to keep moving to find food. What would they be able to keep and take along if they could have only a few possessions? Discuss the idea that today women can do almost any job in our culture, but in many Native American cultures, certain jobs were only women's jobs and certain jobs were only men's jobs. Point out that the women usually put up the tipis made from 15 to 30 hides. Poles were put up and hides draped over them and staked into the ground. Provide copies of reproducible page 45 to students and ask them to describe their lives as Plains Native Americans. Encourage students to share their work with the class.

NATIVE AMERICANS OF THE SOUTHWEST
····· Class Activity ·····

Review with the students the ways the Northwest Coast Native Americans used the forests and waters, and the Plains Native Americans used the buffalo. Then review the natural resources of desert regions with students. Encourage them to name strategies the Southwestern Native Americans could have used to survive in the desert (example: farm near rivers). Discuss how modern day farmers use irrigation to water crops, using pumps and pipes to get the water onto the land. Ask students to suggest ways the Native Americans might have irrigated their crops, even though they did not have pipes. (They could dig ditches to bring water to crops.)

Provide copies of reproducible page 46 to students and invite them to find out about the homes of the Southwest Native Americans. Afterward ask students to compare the homes of these Native Americans with the homes of tribes living on the Northwest coast and on the prairies.

THE NAVAJO
····· Class Activity ·····

Explain that the Navajo people moved from place to place before they settled into farming. They probably learned farming from their neighbors. Corn became a very important crop and played an important role in their spiritual lives. They also began raising sheep that were useful for the wool, which the women wove into beautiful blankets. Point out that some people believe they learned weaving and how to make beautiful silver and turquoise jewelry from neighboring Indian groups.

Invite students to tell what they already know about the Navajo. If any have visited a Navajo reservation, ask them to describe their experiences. Tell students that today the Navajo are the largest group of Native Americans in the United States.

Provide copies of reproducible page 47 to students and ask them to read it and complete the chart. Afterward discuss the beliefs of the Southwest's Native Americans and how they were similar and different from those of other groups.

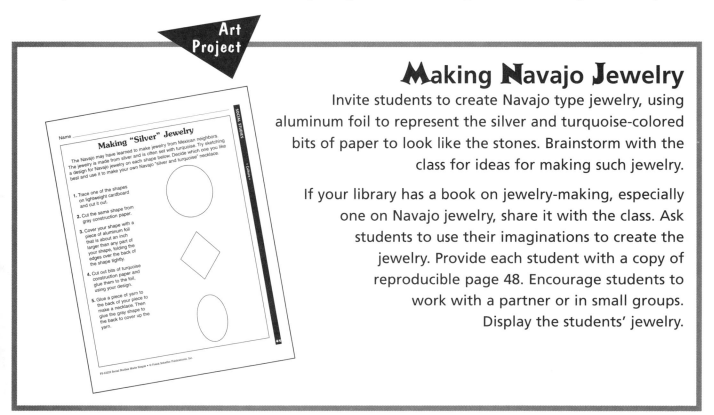

Designing and Weaving Blankets

Provide graph paper to students and invite them to design blankets or just Navajo patterns. They can decorate folders or actually weave the designs. Provide a piece of construction paper, approximately 9″ × 12″ in size. Use black paper if possible because it provides a good background for a design. Have students fold the paper in half and cut slits, one half inch apart. The slits should be cut, beginning at the fold, until they are a half inch from the edge. Tell students not to cut all the way through. Have students cut strips of various colors, such as yellow, red, brown and tan, orange, and black from construction paper. Ask them to use the strips to weave their patterns, using the designs they created, or just make a repeated color pattern into a mat. Have students glue the strips at the end to make the mat more permanent.

STORIES AND STORYTELLING

Class Activity

Model storytelling for the students. Then invite them to choose a Native American myth from the Southwest that they have read or heard and use it for storytelling. Remind them to practice the telling of the story.

Making Navajo Jewelry

Invite students to create Navajo type jewelry, using aluminum foil to represent the silver and turquoise-colored bits of paper to look like the stones. Brainstorm with the class for ideas for making such jewelry.

If your library has a book on jewelry-making, especially one on Navajo jewelry, share it with the class. Ask students to use their imaginations to create the jewelry. Provide each student with a copy of reproducible page 48. Encourage students to work with a partner or in small groups. Display the students' jewelry.

Writing a Native American Report

1. Decide on a Native American group.

2. Find books and encyclopedias.

3. Try to find information about each of the topics below. As you read, take notes.

4. When you have all of the information, write your report in your own words.

5. Plan and practice telling your report. Then give the report in class.

Tribe _____ Location _____

Type of homes_____

Foods and how they got the foods_____

Clothing types and materials _____

Beliefs and/or religion _____

Customs and ceremonies _____

Arts and crafts_____

Music, dance, and recreation (games, fun, etc.) _____

Warfare (if any)_____

Famous persons or events_____

Try This! Write a poem, song, or story about your tribe.
Make a diorama, model, chart, poster, or mural.

FS-23223 Social Studies Made Simple ▪ © Frank Schaffer Publications, Inc.

Northwest Coast Native Americans

Food From the Waters

The Chinook, Haida, Nootka, Tlinglet, Tsimshian, and Kwakiutl lived in the Northwest.

The Kwakiutl, who lived in what is now Canada, used the oceans, rivers, and forests to get shelter, food, and clothing. The sea and rivers provided clams, crabs, mussels, seaweed, cod, herring, halibut, and salmon. Seals, sea lions, otters, and porpoises provided both food and fur for clothing. When they had extra food, they dried it for the winter.

The Kwakiutl believed that all things in nature were related. When the salmon swam upstream to lay eggs, the Kwakiutl believed the fish came to feed their people. The Kwakiutl saved the salmon bones and returned them to the water so the fish would grow new bodies and return next year. They also used waterways for canoe travel.

Write words in each box that go with the title. Tell how the Kwakiutl used each one for food or clothing.

From the Waters

Fish	Other Seafood	Mammals

Help From the Forests

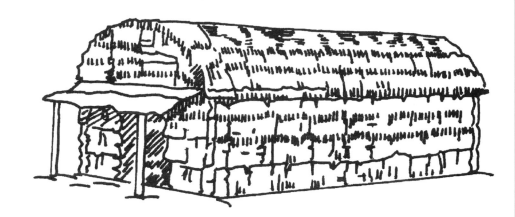

The Kwakiutl picked and ate berries and hunted and trapped animals from the forests. They used wood for building long houses and canoes, and for making bows and arrows, fish hooks, storage chests, toys, and dishes. Masks and rattles for ceremonies and huge totem poles were carved from wood. The totem pole told the story or history of the family.

The Kwakiutl sang to the trees to thank them for their gifts. They used cedar bark for making rope, mats, and clothing. Cedar wood was also a favorite for building long houses. Three or more related families sometimes shared a long house, which was built in a row with other long houses facing the sea.

(continued on page 36)

FS-23223 Social Studies Made Simple ▪ © Frank Schaffer Publications, Inc.

Name _____

Write words or phrases in each oval to show how the Native Americans of the northwest coast used the forests to meet their needs.

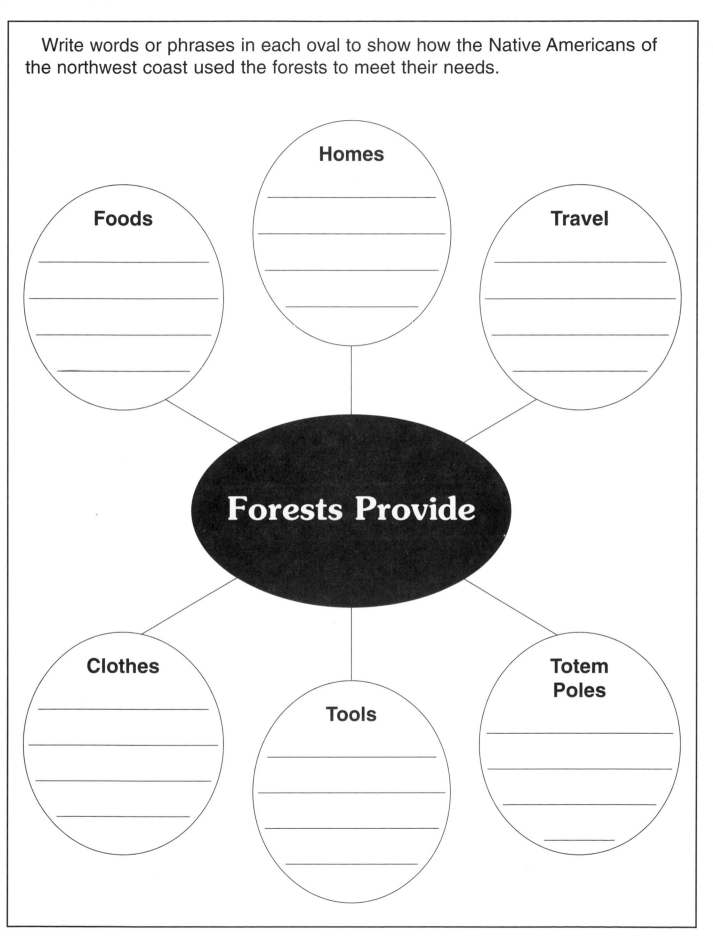

Making a Totem Pole

Study pictures of totem poles in books. Then follow the directions to make your own totem pole.

1. Use a 5″ × 7″ index card or piece of tagboard.

2. Have pieces of construction paper cut in 1 1/2″ × 5″ strips. Have at least five strips of different colors.

3. Roll the card into a seven-inch tube and tape it down the back.

4. Choose five animals for your pole.

5. On each strip of paper, draw a face in the middle. Wrap the strips around the tube and glue them in place, starting with the bottom strip and overlapping each one by a bit.

6. Add noses, ears, "arms" to your totem pole with scraps of construction paper.

Try This!

Make up a story explaining the figures on your totem pole.

Name _____

Making a Mask

Masks were carved from wood and showed creatures from ancient stories. Masks were worn for ceremonies, acting out stories, and dances. Follow the directions below to make your own mask.

1. Study pictures of Native American masks in books. Then make a mask using the shape below.

2. Paint designs on your mask with tempera and glue on features made from construction paper.

3. When the mask is dry, cut slits as shown in the sample by dotted lines.

4. Overlap the pieces and glue or staple in place to give your mask shape.

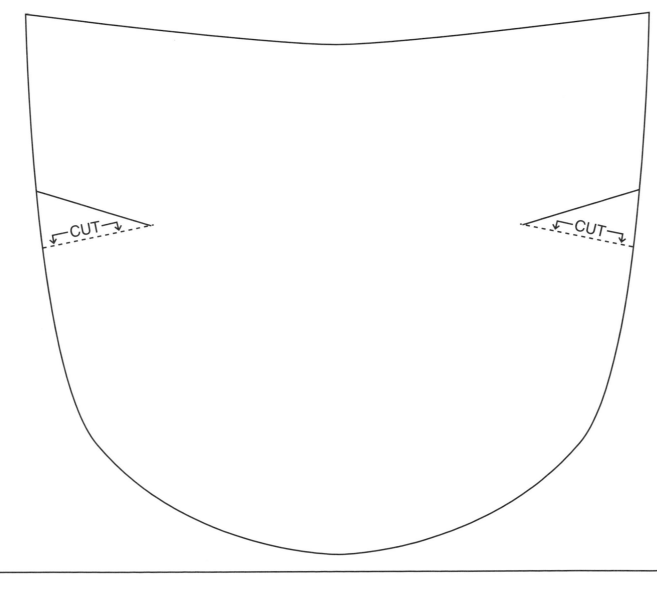

Spotlight On:
The Plains Native Americans

For many years, Native Americans who lived on the plains had to hunt buffalo on foot. The Cheyenne moved around, following buffalo herds. When the Spanish brought horses to the Americas about 250 years ago, Native Americans began to use them to hunt buffalo and to carry heavy loads.

Because Native Americans depended on the buffalo to survive, they lived in movable houses called tipis so they could follow the buffalo. The buffalo provided food, clothing, tools, and shelter. Hides were made into dresses, shirts, robes, and shoes. Small bones were carved into sewing needles. Large bones became sled runners. Buffalo fat, mixed with meat, nuts, and honey, made pemmican, a food that could be stored for a long time.

Tell how the plains Native Americans used the parts of the buffalo below:

Hides _____

_____

Meat and fat _____

_____

Bones _____

_____

How did their lives change when they got horses? _____

_____

_____

_____

_____

_____

Preparing Buffalo Hides

Buffalo hides were important to Plains Native Americans. Their tipis and clothing came from buffalo hides. Preparing the hides and making them ready to use was hard work.

While the hide was fresh, it was stretched on a rack or pegged to the ground. Women scraped the fat and flesh from the hide and then soaked it in water. After several days of soaking, the women scraped off the hair and stretched the hide again. Then they rubbed the hide with a mixture of sand and animal brains. The hide dried stiff and hard.

To make it softer, women rubbed and folded the hides over and over again. When the hide was soft enough to work, they used buffalo-bone needles to sew it into clothes, shoes, and tipis. Sometimes the women added designs using natural dyes.

Step by Step

List the steps that went into making the hides ready to sew. Put the steps in order.

1. _____
   _____

2. _____

3. _____
   _____

4. _____
   _____

5. _____

6. _____
   _____

7. _____

Mini Tipi Village

To make a tipi, Native Americans tied poles together to make a stand. Then they covered the poles with animal hides. To make your mini tipi, follow the steps below.

1. Use the pattern to cut out the tipi shape from a paper bag.

2. Decorate the tipi.

3. Roll the decorated tipi into a cone. Glue the edge with dots behind the other edge. Bend out the flaps at the top to make a smoke hole.

4. Tape or glue toothpicks inside, to look like tipi poles.

5. Put your tipi together with those of your classmates to make a village.

Name _____

Making Buffalo-Hide Crafts

1. Bring a large grocery sack to school. Cut off the bottom of the sack.

2. Cut along the seam (the overlapped part) to open the bag.

3. Cut out a large hide shape. (Your teacher can show you how.)

4. Dampen the bag with water and crumple it into a ball over and over for about ten minutes. It needs to feel soft like cloth.

5. Let the "hide" dry. Then decorate it with Indian designs or with pictures of a buffalo hunt. You can use crayons, markers, or paint.

6. Hang the hides around your room.

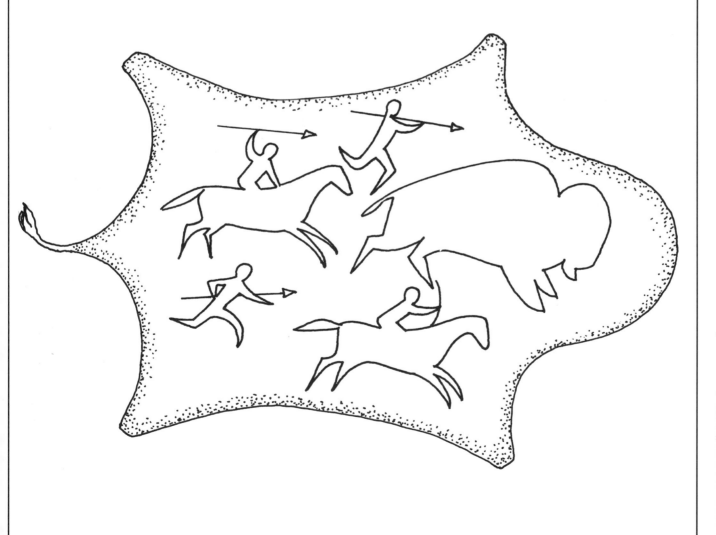

Making a Parfleche

Plains Native Americans often carried things in a pouch made of hide. It was called a parfleche. To make a parfleche, soften a bag as you did for the buffalo hide, but do not cut it into a hide shape. Then follow the directions and use the picture below.

1. Cut out a large rectangle, any size you wish.

2. Fold each side, until it looks like the picture.

3. Punch or cut holes as shown. Use string or twine to tie it closed.

4. Decorate your parfleche.

5. Think about what the Native Americans might have carried in parfleches. What can you carry in yours?

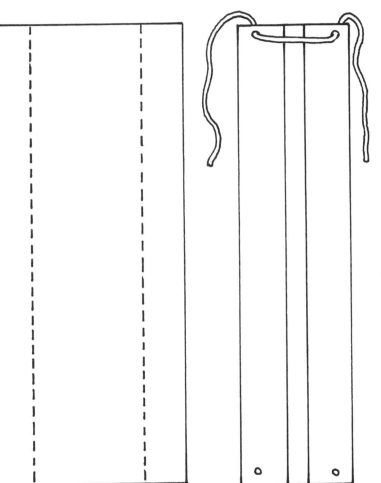

Native American Ceremonies

When the Kwakiutl raised a totem pole, they wore beautifully carved masks. A speechmaker told stories about the history of the family that owned the totem pole. At the ceremonies, people sang, used carved rattles, danced, and feasted. After the ceremonies, there may have been a potlatch where the person who invited the others gave gifts to the guests.

The Cheyenne held medicine dances, asking for help from the powers of nature to the cycle of nature in balance. The medicine man and a woman retold a myth about the spirit, Roaring Thunder, who taught them a dance that brought life back to the earth after a time of little rainfall. A tent stood for the mountains and a decorated tree was a symbol of the cycle of nature. The ceremony lasted several days. The people danced and feasted.

Complete the chart below with information about Native Americans celebrations.

Event	How the Kwakiutl Celebrated

Event	How the Cheyenne Celebrated

My Life as a Native American of the Plains

Imagine that you are a Native American living on the plains before the pioneers came.

Complete the sentences below, telling what your life was like.

1. I would have lived in (tell about the area and what the land was like) _____

_____

_____

2. I made my home from _____ and called it a _____.

I needed this kind of home because _____

_____

3. I used these natural resources _____

_____

4. I wore clothes made mostly from _____

5. I had ceremonies such as _____

_____

6. My parents and I used tools or instruments

such as _____ that might

have been made from _____

_____

Name _____

Living in the Southwest

The Navajo named the earth Changing Woman. Navajo myths said Changing Woman gave the Navajo their first hogan, a one-room house made of shells and turquoise.

The Navajo made similar homes from mud and logs. The hogans were good homes for the hot Southwestern climate. Hogans had no windows to allow heat and cold to enter, and the hogan's door always faced the rising sun in the east. Inside the hogan, women sat on the north side, men on the south, and guests on the west side, across from the door.

A cooking fire in the center of the hogan was built under a hole in the roof that let the smoke escape. Family members slept on sheepskins around the fire.

On the diagram below, tell who or what was in each place inside of the hogan.

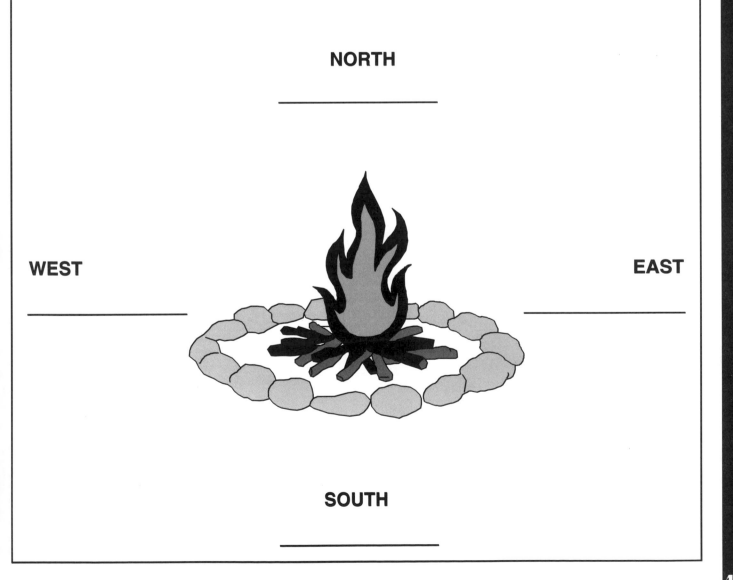

NORTH

_____

WEST _____   **EAST** _____

SOUTH

_____

Southwest Myths and Legends

Navajo legends say that Changing Woman taught the Navajo to grow corn, Spider Woman taught them to weave, and the Wind People taught them to make sand paintings.

Changing Woman was honored in Navajo ceremonies and corn is still an important part of the Navajo diet.

Even today, the Navajo weave beautiful blankets from wool that they shear from their flocks of sheep. They use dyes from plants and berries to color the wool before they weave it.

Although Navajo sand paintings are beautiful, the Navajo believed that the Wind People did not want the paintings to be saved because people might fight over them. The sand paintings were swept away after about 12 hours. That was a long enough time, the Navajo believed, for the paintings and chants to help make people well.

On the chart below, tell who the myths said taught the Navajo the skills they used so well. You can add other ideas too.

Craft or skill	Who taught the skill
Growing Corn	
Weaving	
Sand Painting	

FS-23223 Social Studies Made Simple ▪ © Frank Schaffer Publications, Inc.

Making "Silver" Jewelry

The Navajo may have learned to make jewelry from Mexican neighbors. The jewelry is made from silver and is often set with turquoise. Try sketching a design for Navajo jewelry on each shape below. Decide which one you like best and use it to make your own Navajo "silver and turquoise" necklace.

1. Trace one of the shapes on lightweight cardboard and cut it out.

2. Cut the same shape from gray construction paper.

3. Cover your shape with a piece of aluminum foil that is about an inch larger than any part of your shape, folding the edges over the back of the shape tightly.

4. Cut out bits of turquoise construction paper and glue them to the foil, using your design.

5. Glue a piece of yarn to the back of your piece to make a necklace. Then glue the gray shape to the back to cover up the yarn.

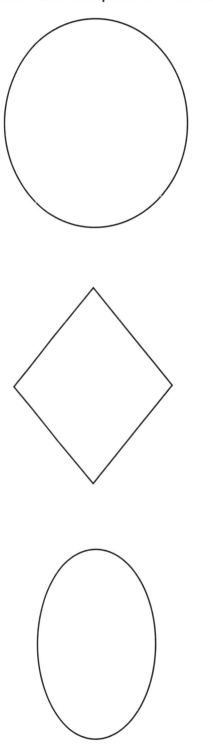

History

In this unit, students will discover the historical roots of the United States by participating in this selection of historical activities.

SETTLING THE LAND: THE NORTHEAST

Locate England on a large political world map. Tell students that England is considered a part of the European continent. Provide copies of a blank world map to students. Ask them to color in England and draw the route of the Pilgrims. Review the story of Columbus and then ask students to color Spain on the map. Tell students to save their maps because they will work with them later on.

Discuss how sailing ships were different from modern ships. If possible, take students to your school yard or a nearby playground and ask them to mark off the length and the width of the *Mayflower*. Invite children from other classes to join your students "on the *Mayflower*," so they can note the amount of room the Pilgrims had to stand and sleep when staying in confined quarters for 65 days.

SIXTY-FIVE DAYS AT SEA

Ask students to imagine that they are Pilgrim children and to write about their journey on the *Mayflower*. Before students begin, ask them to think how they might feel if they were going to move to a new land, leave their friends, sail across the ocean for many months, live below deck in a damp, dark ship, and so on. Suggest they make a list of the good things (for example: worshipping as they saw fit, having more land) as well as the bad things related to the voyage. Have students read their stories to the class.

Provide as many books about the Pilgrims as possible. Have students work with a partner and use an encyclopedia and other books to find out more about the *Mayflower*. Provide a copy of reproducible page 54 to each student. Ask students to read the page and fill in the chart.

SURVIVING IN AMERICA ..... Class Activity .....

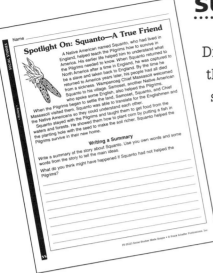

Discuss the things the Pilgrims had to do to try to survive. Ask students to think of things that might have caused only about half of the Pilgrims to survive the first winter. Encourage them to speculate on whether more people would have survived if they had the medicines of today. Ask students how the first months would have been different if the Pilgrims had arrived in the spring or summer months instead of December. Provide copies of reproducible page 55 to students and remind them that before writing a summary, they need to identify the main ideas. Discuss how Squanto might have felt living in England.

A THANKSGIVING FEAST! ..... Class Activity .....

Invite students to plan a mini Thanksgiving feast as a class. Have them organize into groups to share the work and to bring food such as fruit to class. If possible, bake cornbread with the class and make a fruit salad from fruit children bring to share. Ask students how their own sharing is similar to the Pilgrim's sharing what they had with the Native Americans who helped them so much to survive in the New World. Invite students to chart the ways the Native Americans helped Pilgrims (learning to hunt, fish, plant, and use fish for fertilizer).

Have students research the types of games the Pilgrims and Native Americans played and play some of them at the feast. Ask students to draw or list the food eaten by the Pilgrims (wild turkey, partridges, ducks, geese, seafood, deer, pumpkins, corn, cornbread, pudding, berries, types of salad). Have them circle the things they have eaten.

WRITING A THANKSGIVING PLAY ..... Group Activity .....

Ask the class to write a play about Thanksgiving as a group, making up dialogue for the characters. Read aloud the book, *The First Thanksgiving Feast,* by Joan Anderson, to give children ideas for dialogue and costumes. It has photographs of Plymouth Plantation. (See the Resources page.) Have the class perform their play for other classes and/or parents. As a modern day activity, have small groups plan a Thanksgiving feast, writing a menu and making invitations for friends and family to attend the feast. They need to include the time, place, and perhaps mention the activities.

For another activity, make a chart with the students. On one side of the chart, list the reasons the Pilgrims who survived had to be thankful. On the other side, list the reasons we have to be thankful.

SPOTLIGHT ON THE WILDERNESS ROAD

Class Activity

Locate the Appalachian Mountains on a map of the United States. Discuss why the mountains were a major barrier to people traveling in small wagons. Provide copies of reproducible page 56 to students and ask them to complete the page. To extend the activity, discuss why the settlement of America was dangerous. Challenge students to think about what settlement on the moon would require today. Ask how the settlement of America would be like the settlement of the moon. List students' responses.

MAKE IT FOR YOURSELF

Group Activity

Discuss what kinds of things the settlers had to make for themselves. Have students brainstorm, in small groups, for things the settlers would have needed. Challenge students to prioritize the items, deciding what to make first, second, and so on. Have the groups meet as a whole group and compare their ideas.

COMPARING HOMES

Class Activity

Encourage a student who owns building logs, such as Lincoln Logs™, to bring a few to school so the children can see how they were notched to fit together. Ask students if they think hand-notched logs fit together as well as machine-crafted toy logs. Discuss the need for filling the gaps with mortar, mud, and moss. Ask students to compare a one-room log cabin to their homes. Have the students fold a piece of paper in half, listing things about their homes on one side and things about log cabins on the other.

FOLLOWING THE EXAMPLE OF NATIVE AMERICANS

Class Activity

Review how the Native Americans used the resources of the land. Discuss why the Pilgrims needed to do the same, using the wood and foods from the forests, growing food on the land, getting fish and other seafood from the waters, using animal skins for clothing, and collecting herbs for medicine.

COVERED WAGONS

Class Activity

Ask students to research and discuss covered wagons and wagon trains. Display a picture and have students speculate as to why covered wagons were called *prairie schooners.* Ask students to draw or paint pictures of a wagon train crossing the prairie.

Provide copies of reproducible page 58 to the class. Ask the students to make miniature wagons and put all the wagons together to form a circle. Discuss why this was the safest way to stop at night. Ask students where in the wagon train they would like to have their wagon and why. (The last wagon would have a problem if it breaks down; it would receive dust from all the other wagons. The first wagon would be the one to encounter dangerous conditions first. Middle wagons would have to endure dust and keep pace with the leaders.)

FS-23223 Social Studies Made Simple ▪ © Frank Schaffer Publications, Inc.

PIONEERS MOVE INLAND····· Class Activity ·····

Explain that as many more people arrived in America, some began to feel America was getting crowded. Others wanted inexpensive or free land. With the students' input, list the dangers pioneers faced as they moved inland, away from the coast, to Kentucky and other areas. Ask students which they would rather have been, a Pilgrim or a pioneer moving inland. Ask them to give reasons. Provide copies of reproducible page 57 and ask students to complete the page.

A JOURNEY BY WAGON····· Class Activity ·····

Invite students to research the wagons, finding out the size and once again measuring off the amount of space in a wagon. Ask them to list the things they would have needed to take. Encourage them to decide to think of the one thing (nothing electrical, of course) that they would have taken along as their personal possession in the wagon. Help students understand how people felt leaving homes, possessions, and friends and family behind, perhaps never to see them again, as they started into the wilderness.

Have students write a journal entry about a day or week in the wagon train. Invite them to read their stories aloud. Suggest combining all of them into a class journal.

Art Project

Quilts

Bring books about quilts and quilting to class and invite students to look through or read them. Provide copies of reproducible page 59 to students and ask them to design a quilt square using patterned cloth, wallpaper, or wrapping paper.

Put the squares together on a piece of butcher paper or on the bulletin board. The butcher paper quilt can be saved and hung for visitors. If you use wrapping paper, you can make a different group quilt for each season, so you will have several to hang on special days. The first quilt square can be a simple four-patch, while later ones can be nine patches (nine 3" x 3" blocks), which are shown frequently in quilt books. Ask students to copy a design or make up their own design. Have students show the design to you before gluing the pieces down for your suggestions.

FRACTIONS

Use the quilts as an introduction to the study of fractions. On the four patch, each section is 1/4 of the whole. Students may use the same pattern for two parts, or they could cut a section in half, possibly diagonally, making a square into a triangle which is now 1/8 of the whole. Help students analyze their squares and help them find what fractional part is occupied by each print or plain color, and so on. With the entire group, find the fractional part each square plays in your whole quilt, too.

MOVING WESTWARD

Have students speculate why settlers would keep moving west into unexplored lands. Using their maps, students should identify the trails, showing the Wilderness Trail, the Santa Fe Trail, the Oregon Trail, and its branch, the California Trail. Provide copies of reproducible page 60 to students and ask them to study the types of people who mainly traveled each trail.

HEALTH AMONG PIONEERS

Challenge students to find out what diseases people contracted while traveling (scurvy from lack of fresh fruits and vegetables, cholera from the germs in dirty water). Discuss how we protect ourselves from such diseases.

Students are fascinated by the short life spans of people in history as compared to people of today, such as their grandparents. Discuss how science and medicine and the availability of doctors changed the lives and life spans.

RAILROADS

Encourage students to study the ways the railroads changed our country, making it easier for people to travel, move, ship goods, and so on. Ask the class to compare railroad travel to airplane travel. Discuss why our world seems much smaller than the world of the pioneers.

Art Project

A Then and Now Mural

Invite students to work in groups to plan and create a mural showing life long ago and life today. Ask students to pay special attention to means of transportation.

FS-23223 Social Studies Made Simple ▪ © Frank Schaffer Publications, Inc.

Settling the Northeast—The Pilgrims

After a 65-day journey across the Atlantic Ocean, the Pilgrims settled in Plymouth in December of 1620. They came because they wanted to be able to worship God in their own way.

They had hoped to join settlers already in Jamestown, but they landed too far north.

While the women and children stayed on the *Mayflower,* the men went ashore to hunt for food. They dug holes in hills for shelter. Eventually, they were able to clear enough land to build homes. Before the next summer arrived, though, about half of the 102 people who began the journey had died.

In the spring, they met the friendly Wampanoag Native Americans and Squanto. They taught them to hunt, fish, and grow beans, pumpkins, and corn, and to use fish when planting things, much as we use fertilizer today.

Fill in the chart telling how the Pilgrim's problems were solved.

1. They wanted to worship in their own way.	
2. They landed in winter and had no homes and little food.	
3. They didn't know much about farming in their new land.	
4. They didn't have many skills for finding food from the land.	

Spotlight On: Squanto—A True Friend

A Native American named Squanto, who had lived in England, helped teach the Pilgrims how to survive in America. His earlier life helped him to understand what the Pilgrims needed to know. When Squanto returned to North America after a time in England, he was captured to be a slave and taken back to England. By the time he returned to America years later, his people had all died from a sickness. Wampanoag Chief Massasoit welcomed Squanto to his village. Samoset, another Native American who spoke some English, also helped the Pilgrims.

When the Pilgrims began to settle the land, Samoset, Squanto, and Chief Massasoit visited them. Squanto was able to translate for the Englishmen and the Native Americans so they could understand each other.

Squanto stayed with the Pilgrims and taught them to get food from the waters and forests. He showed them how to plant corn by putting a fish in the planting hole with the seed to make the soil richer. Squanto helped the Pilgrims survive in their new home.

Writing a Summary

Write a summary of the story about Squanto. Use your own words and some words from the story to tell the main ideas.

What do you think might have happened if Squanto had not helped the Pilgrims?

_____

_____

_____

_____

_____

_____

_____

Name _____

Over the Mountains

As more people came to America, they began to move farther and farther west. Traders and fur trappers first explored western lands. They looked for good trapping areas. When they returned with stories of rich lands in the west, pioneers began to go west, too. In time, some settled on the Great Plains. Others moved all the way to the west coast.

The trip was difficult from the start. Pioneers had to cross the Appalachian Mountains, but there were no roads wide enough for their wagons.

Daniel Boone and a crew cleared land and "built" the Wilderness Road across the mountains. About 30 men helped clear land from Virginia to Kentucky. Boone marked the trees, blazing a trail. His crew followed, clearing the underbrush and trees. In 1774, the trail was finished. Settlers packed their belongings into wagons or on horseback and set off on the Wilderness Road.

Without bridges, streams and rivers were difficult to cross. Wagon wheels got stuck in the mud or broke and were hard to repair. Sometimes, Native Americans attacked the wagons. Still, the Wilderness Road carried thousands of settlers across the Appalachians.

Answer the questions about the Wilderness Road.

1. Tell why the Wilderness Road was so badly needed. _____

_____

_____

2. How was it created? _____

_____

_____

3. Tell about the problems settlers had even after the road was opened.

_____

_____

_____

Moving Inland

Not long after the Pilgrims came to America, others came and settled in towns and cities that grew up along the East Coast. Some people moved inland and built log cabins and started farms. If farmers grew extra food, they sold it in the cities.

There were no stores in the wilderness so settlers had to make almost everything they needed. Using axes, settlers chopped down trees and built cabins of notched logs. They also used the wood for wagons, homes, tools, cradles, furniture, and dishes. The settlers grew their own food once the Delaware Native Americans taught them to grow corn, beans, and squash. Medicine came from herbs that the Delaware helped settlers find.

Since the settlers often lived far apart, they made a special event out of getting together. Sometimes people traveled from miles around to help new settlers raise a cabin. When the job was done, there might be singing, story telling, or a *quilting bee,* where women got together to make quilts to keep their families warm during the winter.

Comparing Periods in History

Write as many ways as you can think of that life was similar for the Pilgrims and the Pioneers. Then write the ways that life was different for them.

Ways Life Was Similar (somewhat alike)	Ways Life Was Different

Making a Covered Wagon Model

1. Cut out the wagon shape along the solid lines.

2. Fold the sides, front, and back up on the dotted lines. Fold the flaps and glue them under the front and back parts to make an open box shape.

3. Cut out four wheels and glue them to the sides of the wagon, or attach them with paper fasteners.

4. Bend four or five pipe cleaners into a curve. Glue or tape them inside the wagon to make an arch.

5. Cut a piece of white cloth or crepe paper to fit over the pipe-cleaner arch, covering just a tiny part of the wagon sides. Glue this top in place.

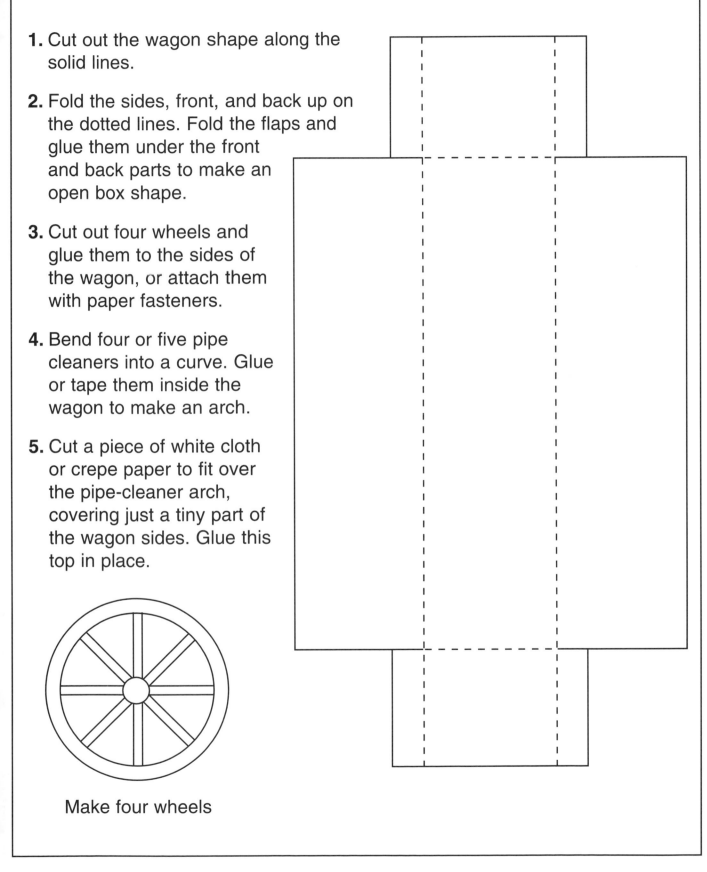

Make four wheels

Making a Quilt

One of the activities that pioneer women enjoyed was quilt making. Maybe you know someone today who enjoys making or collecting quilts. The pioneer women used fabric scraps and their own designs to make their quilts.

Design your own quilt square on the page below. Combine your square with the squares of your classmates to make a class "quilt."

1. Use the four-patch square below. Decide on a pattern. Use one you have seen or make up your own pattern.

2. Cut pieces of wrapping paper, wallpaper, or real fabric.

3. Lay the pieces in the places you plan to paste them. Have your teacher look at your design before you glue the pieces in place.

Name _____

On to California

After the Wilderness Road opened in 1774, it was only a matter of time before other routes led settlers farther and farther west. Land was cheap in the wide open west. News of gold, silver, and other minerals drew prospectors. Some went west to buy and sell goods to homesteaders and prospectors.

Traveling to the far west was even more difficult than crossing the Appalachian Mountains. Dangerous rivers and high mountains blocked the wagon's way. Finding food and clean water on such a long journey was hard, especially in the Southwestern deserts. Mountain passes filled with snow. Each trail held dangers for those who packed their wagons to start a new life in the far west.

The Santa Fe Trail opened in 1821. It began in Independence, Missouri; crossed the plains; and turned southwest through the Cimarron Desert, ending in Santa Fe, New Mexico. Later, it continued to Los Angeles, California.

Families used the Oregon Trail to move west in search of land for homes and farms. The Oregon Trail also began at Independence, Missouri, but it went northwest over the Great Plains. It passed through the Rocky Mountains at South Pass, and travelers could only use that part of the trail in summer when it was free of snow. Wagon trains then continued on to Oregon or turned south to the California Trail.

For each trail listed below, tell where it started, where it ended, and what made it dangerous or difficult.

The Wilderness Road _____

_____

The Santa Fe Trail _____

_____

The Oregon and California Trails _____

_____

Try This! On the back of this sheet tell which trail you would take if you were a pioneer. Tell why you picked that trail.

Spotlight On: Abraham Lincoln

When Abraham Lincoln was born on February 12, 1809, the United States was only 23 years old. By the time Abraham Lincoln became president in 1860, the young country was in danger of splitting apart.

As a young man, Lincoln traveled on the Mississippi River delivering farm products. At the time, many of the large plantations in the South used enslaved Africans to do the heavy farm work. The enslaved people were bought and sold. Many people in the North thought that it was wrong to buy and sell people as slaves. Lincoln agreed. All over the country, people argued about slavery. In 1858, Lincoln ran for senator. He debated with Stephen Douglas about slavery. Lincoln lost the election, but he became well known in America. Two years later, Lincoln won the vote for president.

After the election, the slavery arguments grew louder. The South threatened to split the United States. When some states in the South formed the Confederate States of America, Lincoln would not let the country split up. In 1861, the North and South went to war.

In 1863, Lincoln freed the slaves in the South. In 1864, when the voters gave him another term as president, he promised to bring the country back together. When the war ended on April 9, 1865, though, Lincoln would live just six more days. He was shot by an actor, John Wilkes Booth, while attending a play. He died on April 15, 1865.

Write the correct date beside each fact.

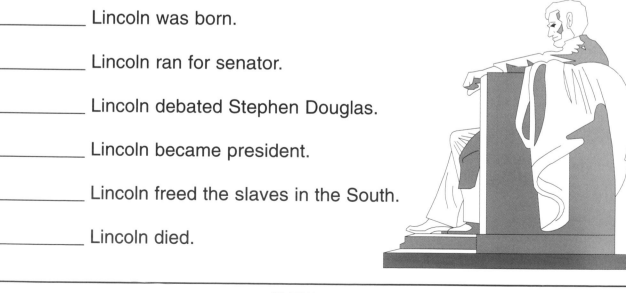

_____ Lincoln was born.

_____ Lincoln ran for senator.

_____ Lincoln debated Stephen Douglas.

_____ Lincoln became president.

_____ Lincoln freed the slaves in the South.

_____ Lincoln died.

Economics

As the farms of settlers in America grew and people produced more than they could use, they traded with each other. Today the goods and services produced in the United States are sold all over the world and countries are each other's trading partners. People work at specific jobs and buy the goods and services they want and need.

MAKING GOODS AND PROVIDING SERVICES

Group Activity

Explain to students the two basic kinds of jobs people hold: making goods or providing services. Make two lists with students, one of jobs people hold making goods and the other of jobs that are service jobs. Then form three groups. Help one group to find out what kinds of products are made or grown in your local area; help another group to find out what products are grown or manufactured in your state. Help the third group find goods and services traded between the United States and other countries. Suggest that students talk to parents and other adults and read labels on clothing and on products in stores, including cans of food. The local Chamber of Commerce can provide information about what goods are produced in your state and local area.

JOBS IN THE LOCAL AREA

Class Activity

MECHANIC
Heavy equipment repair shop seeking Technician with wide range of equipment knowledge for shop & field repairs. Excellent wage and benefit package for a highly motivated individual. Call 555-0000.

Invite students to find out more about jobs in your area. Explain that they can list jobs of family members, neighbors, friends, and others, such as employees in shopping centers, doctors, dentists, and teachers, that they know about. Ask students to combine their lists. Have students look over the lists of jobs and think about what jobs are most plentiful in your area. Read some help wanted ads to the class from your local newspaper. Ask why there are seldom job ads for farmers but often ads for service jobs. Help students to understand that today's workers need different skills from those of their grandparents and great-grandparents because of changes in science and technology.

ECONOMIC CYCLE

Class Activity

Make a chart showing the economic cycle: people move to an area—people need supplies—businesses begin to provide what people need—business need employees—employees need more products and homes, and so on, and eventually a city grows. Discuss the chart with students.

Chart the advances in transporting products from a little family wagon, to the current methods of sending goods by trucks, trains, ships and barges, and airplanes.

SPECIALIZATION

Call students' attention to our present-day specialization and the huge changes that have taken place from early days when people raised their own food and made most things they needed. Brainstorm a list with students of the things the settlers did not have, such as electricity, running water inside their homes, TVs and radios, tractors, cars, airplanes, trucks, large ships, and so on. Discuss with students how modern science and technology contributed to the changes and to the specialization in jobs.

Name _____

Business Changes

Long ago, new settlers from Europe were lucky to grow enough food for their families. As farms got bigger, some farmers raised more food than they needed. They began to trade food for other things.

Today, people do not make or grow all the things they use. Instead, they earn money at jobs and use the money to buy what they need. Products come from all over the world. The fastest way to ship them is by airplane. Shipping by airplane is expensive, though, and the product still needs to travel, probably by truck, to the store that sells it.

Trains carry heavy products and shipping costs less by train, but trains are slower than airplanes. Things shipped by train still have to be trucked to stores for sale.

Although shipping by truck costs less than shipping by plane or train, trucks are slower than planes and carry less than trains. Trucks can bring things right to the store.

Ships and barges can only go where there are waterways and are often slow, but they can carry heavy loads for a low cost.

Write the good and bad things about each kind of transportation under the headings.

Planes	Trucks
Trains	Ships

FS-23223 Social Studies Made Simple ■ © Frank Schaffer Publications, Inc.

Provide copies of reproducible page 64 and ask students to complete the page. Discuss with students how transportation of goods has changed the way people live today.

Make a graph of products, such as cars or cameras, that are owned by families of students, showing the countries which produce the products. Talk about how the cars not made in our country were sent. Your students may wish to survey other classes so your graph will represent a larger number.

TRANSPORTING GOODS

Invite one group of students to research the different advantages of each method of transporting goods. Ask another group to make a poster on how train, cars, or planes have changed. Encourage them to include information on such people as the Wright brothers or Amelia Earhart.

Science Project

TECHNOLOGY AND INVENTIONS

Encourage some students to research inventions, such as electricity, and inventors, such as the Wright brothers. Ask other students to report on how things have changed because of such inventions as telephones, electricity, cameras, trains, cars, planes, computers, and so on. Invite students to tell the class what they found.

Discuss with students the changes for the better and the problems, such as pollution, that have increased due to manufacturing and car pollution. Make out a list with students' input on ways people can conserve the resources and help prevent pollution.

Business Changes

Long ago, new settlers from Europe were lucky to grow enough food for their families. As farms got bigger, some farmers raised more food than they needed. They began to trade food for other things.

Today, people do not make or grow all the things they use. Instead, they earn money at jobs and use the money to buy what they need. Products come from all over the world. The fastest way to ship them is by airplane. Shipping by airplane is expensive, though, and the product still needs to travel, probably by truck, to the store that sells it.

Trains carry heavy products and shipping costs less by train, but trains are slower than airplanes. Things shipped by train still have to be trucked to stores for sale.

Although shipping by truck costs less than shipping by plane or train, trucks are slower than planes and carry less than trains. Trucks can bring things right to the store.

Ships and barges can only go where there are waterways and are often slow, but they can carry heavy loads for a low cost.

Write the good and bad things about each kind of transportation under the headings.

Planes	**Trucks**
Trains	**Ships**

Trade with Other Countries

The United States buys and sells products from countries all over the world. When countries buy and sell products from each other, it is called *international trade.* Products sent out of a country to be sold are called *exports.* Products brought into a country are called *imports.*

In your home, neighborhood, and stores, you will probably find products from other countries. Cars and TVs and other electronic products may have been made in other countries. Some packaged foods are imported. Perhaps someone in the stores near your home can tell you about products that come from other countries.

Find out about as many imported products as you can. List the products and countries they came from. Then compare your list with your classmates' lists. Make a chart or bulletin board showing some things we buy from other countries.

Product	Country

Government and Citizenship

In this unit, students will begin to explore the government of the United States and the responsibilities of its citizens. They will look at how the government is organized and what symbols represent the United States government both at home and abroad.

BRANCHES OF GOVERNMENT

Group Activity

Make a chart on the bulletin board showing the three branches of our government. Alongside, display copies of the Constitution, the Bill of Rights, and perhaps the Declaration of Independence.

Form small groups to study each branch of government and report on the qualifications and duties of its members. Encourage students to use textbooks and encyclopedias.

SPOTLIGHT ON GEORGE WASHINGTON

Class Activity

Provide copies of reproducible page 69 to students and ask them to read about George Washington. After completion of the page, discuss Washington's contribution to our country and the sequence activity.

PEOPLE IN GOVERNMENT

Class Activity

As a creative writing assignment, have the students choose the branch they would most like to be a part of, tell how they could become a member of that group, and what they would like to accomplish there.

Provide copies of reproducible page 70 to students. Ask them to do research on their chosen president and present the report to the class. Display the students' work.

CITIZENSHIP

Class Activity

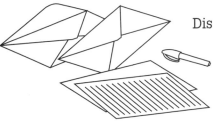

Discuss with students what they think their responsibilities as third-graders are. Ask them how they could practice good citizenship, even as members of their class.

Encourage students to think of causes that are important to them, the community, or people in general and write to their Congressional Representatives and to the president. Post all responses students receive on the bulletin board.

FORMING A SCHOOL GROUP

Form a group with students for various projects such as a special day at school, clean-up the campus day, collecting food for the needy day, and so on. Ask students to name a purpose for setting up the group and have them establish goals for the group. Ask students to decide what they want to accomplish, what each student's role will be, and how they will organize their project. Elect officers and have students tell why they would like to serve in a particular office. Keep track of who has participated, so everyone will have a chance to be involved.

Provide copies of reproducible page 72 to students. Ask them to read and complete the page. Then ask individuals to present their plan for their group.

WHY ARE LAWS NEEDED?

Allow a few minutes when everyone in your class does whatever he or she wants (with limits set for safety, but these should be discussed so students can see the extremes of lawlessness). Then discuss what would happen if there were no traffic rules or no school and playground rules.

Have students decide on a few of the most important rules for your class, as well as consequences for breaking the rules. Help students relate these to laws and our justice system.

RESEARCH A STATE AND A PRESIDENT

See student pages for report forms for researching a state (reproducible page 75) and a president (reproducible page 70.) You many want to study the creation of Washington, D.C., and let students discuss where they think the capital could have been located if it had been established after the whole country had developed.

SPOTLIGHT ON THE WHITE HOUSE

The White House is one of the most important symbols associated with the United States. Help students learn more about this historic building by doing the spotlight activity on reproducible page 74.

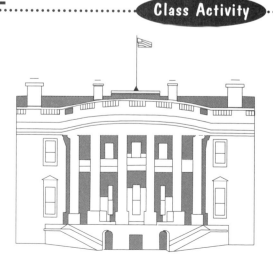

NATIONAL SYMBOLS

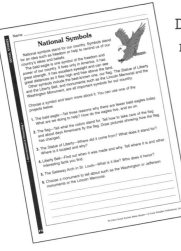

Display books about our national symbols and monuments and ask students to read books about them. Provide copies of reproducible page 73 to students. Ask them to choose a symbol and research it. Encourage them also to research the bald eagle, how its number have dwindled, and what we are doing about it. Discuss the reasons for symbols and how they instill pride. Ask students to find examples of the symbols, such as on coins, seals, etc.

Art Project

State Symbols

Have students do research to find out what some of the symbols of their state are, such as the state bird, flower, tree, and flag. Ask them to draw the symbols and share them with the class. Display students' drawings on the bulletin board.

Provide copies of reproducible page 75 to students to learn more about the symbols of other states and about important people who were born there. Invite students to share their findings and drawings with the class.

OUR NATION'S SONGS

Discuss (and sing) "The Star-Spangled Banner," the meaning of the song, and why it was written. Ask students to find songs from various periods in our history and make a booklet of such songs. Sing a variety of our nation's songs with the class. Discuss the importance of having pride in one's country with the class.

Spotlight On: George Washington, Father of Our Country

George Washington was born in 1732 in Westmoreland County, Virginia. When George was eleven, his father died and George went to live with his half-brother, Lawrence. Lawrence died when George was 20 years old and George became owner of Mount Vernon, his beloved home.

When he was young, George enjoyed math, history, geography, farming, and the military. Later, George used his skill with numbers to learn surveying, the measuring and mapping of lands. He traveled across mountains and rivers and learned to survive in the wilderness. His training helped him when he began his military career in 1752.

His leadership qualities helped him become a member of the Continental Congress and made others respect him. In 1776, when war broke out with the British, he was chosen as commander-in-chief of the Continental Army.

In 1781, when the war was over, our new nation chose George Washington as our first president. After his first term, he was selected to serve for another four years. Three years after he left office, "The Father of Our Country" became ill and died.

Sequence—Putting Things in Order

Put the events in order by writing the letter of the event in the correct space.

A. He became the first president.

B. George was born.

C. George became a surveyor.

D. He became ill and died.

E. He led the Continental Army.

F. He was in the Continental Congress.

1. _____   2. _____   3. _____

4. _____   5. _____   6. _____

FS-23223 Social Studies Made Simple • © Frank Schaffer Publications, Inc.

Name ______________________________

Reporting on a President

Have you ever thought of being president of the United States? Here are the rules for being president. The person must be at least 35 years old. He or she must have been born in the United States and lived here for 14 years.

Decide on one president you would like to study. Use a book about presidents and an encyclopedia. Write a report that uses as many of the topics listed below as possible. Draw a picture of your president in the box below.

President's Name ______________________________

Birthdate ______________________________

Birthplace ______________________________

Occupations (jobs or careers) he had ______________________________

____

Years when he was president ______________________________

Important things that happened when he was in office ______________________________

____

Important things he did while he was in office ______________________________

____

Famous things he said ______________________________

____

____

Other interesting facts about this president ______________________________

____

____

____

SOCIAL STUDIES • Government & Citizenship •

Leadership Skills— Forming a New Group

The United States has had many great leaders. Leaders have skills which make them successful. George Washington was a military and political leader. He worked with soldiers, cheering them up and even buying them food with his own money. He had good ideas for helping the new country get started.

Another leader that helped our country through hard times was Abraham Lincoln. He was called "Honest Abe." He had a wide grin and was good at telling stories. He cared about other people.

Both leaders had goals and worked for these goals. Washington needed to see that the new country was well organized and got off to a good start. Lincoln wanted all people to be free and to keep the states together as one country.

What Makes a Good Leader?

Use the story about two great presidents to find things that made them good leaders. List the things that make good leaders on the lines below.

_____

_____

_____

_____

_____

_____

_____

_____

_____

Forming a Club

It is fun to be part of a country, school, class, and other groups. You may be a member of a scout group or an athletic team. Your school may have a Student Council and clubs for people who like the same things. Here are some things you can do to make your group successful.

1. Decide on a purpose for your group. For example, you may be interested in drawing, collecting something such a baseball cards or shells, or becoming better at a sport.

   The purpose of our group is _____

2. Organization—You need to plan a time and place to meet. You can change these if you need to, as time passes.

   We will meet on (day) _____ at (time) _____

   at (place) _____.

3. You also need to plan activities (what you will do), so members want to join

   the group. Add new activities as the year goes on. We will _____

   _____

4. You will need a leader. For example, you may want someone with good ideas who will listen to your ideas, too. You can share the leadership so many people have a turn. Make a list of people interested in the group and in leadership. Plan a time for your first meeting. Together, set goals, choose a leader, and get started. Make your club interesting and have fun!

Members list

_____

_____

_____

SOCIAL STUDIES

• Government & Citizenship •

National Symbols

National symbols stand for our country. Symbols stand for an idea such as freedom or help to remind us of our country's ideas and beliefs.

The bald eagle is one symbol of the freedom and power of our country. It lives only in America. It has great strength. It has excellent eyesight and can see great distances as it flies high and free above the land.

Other symbols include the best-known one, our flag. The Statue of Liberty and the Liberty Bell, and monuments such as the Lincoln Memorial and the Washington Monument, are all important symbols for our country.

Choose a symbol and learn more about it. You can use one of the projects below.

1. The bald eagle—Tell three reasons why there are fewer bald eagles today. What are we doing to help? How do the eagles live, and so on.

2. The flag—Tell what the colors stand for. Tell how to take care of the flag and about days Americans fly the flag. Draw pictures showing how the flag has changed.

3. The Statue of Liberty—Where did it come from? What does it stand for? Where is it located and why?

4. Liberty Bell—Find out when it was made and why. Tell where it is and other interesting facts you find.

5. The Gateway Arch in St. Louis—What is it like? Who does it honor?

6. Choose a monument to tell about such as the Washington or Jefferson monuments or the Lincoln Memorial.

_____

_____

_____

_____

Spotlight On: The White House

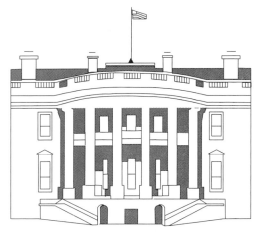

Every president except George Washington lived in the White House. George Washington helped to plan the White House, though. It is our nation's oldest historical building. President John Adams and his family moved into the White House in November of 1800, but the home was not called the White House then.

The building was painted white after the British tried to burn it during the War of 1812. When Harry Truman was president, the White House was updated.

The White House has rooms that are private. The president's family lives in these rooms. Others are used for official events. The East Room is a grand ballroom decorated in gold and white.

Next to the East Room is the Green Room where the president may meet representatives from other countries. The walls are covered with green material and the rug contains a copy of the Presidential Seal. Other rooms are the Blue Room, or "State Parlor," and the State Dining Room.

The Lincoln bedroom contains the huge Lincoln bed and the Red Room may be used for the president to meet his personal guests.

Try This!

Find pictures of the inside of the White House. Draw your favorite room in the space above and share it with the class.

State Report

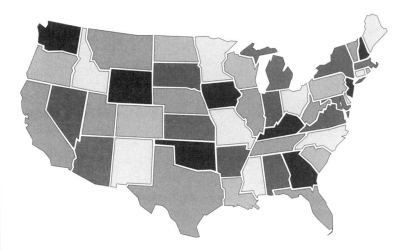

Choose a state other than your own. Use books, encyclopedias, or your computer to find out more about the state. Some states will send information if you write to them. Use this page for ideas. Write a report about the state and share it with your class.

State Name _____

Capital _____

Location _____

Date of Statehood _____

Nickname (if any) _____

State Bird _____

State Flower _____

State Tree _____

- Draw a map of your state. Show the physical features for the state.
- Draw some of the products produced in the state. Write a list of other important products.
- Try to find out about an important person who was born there.
- Tell about places to visit in the state. Make a travel folder to interest people in visiting your state. You may get ideas from travel folders provided by a travel agent.

Answer Key

Page 11

Events chosen will vary.

Page 12

Labels for continents: Africa, Asia, North America, South America, Australia, and Europe. (Antarctica has been omitted.) **Labels for oceans:** Atlantic Ocean, Pacific Ocean, Arctic Ocean, and Indian Ocean. (Antarctic Ocean may be omitted.)

Page 13

1. Oceans change the land through erosion, where land is worn away, or through adding landmass by leaving behind sand, rocks, and crushed shells.

2. People use oceans to get fish and shellfish, to transport goods and people, and for recreation.

Page 14

Students should label Lake Erie, Lake Michigan, Lake Ontario, Lake Superior, and Lake Huron. They should also label the Missouri River, the Mississippi River, the Atlantic Ocean, and the Pacific Ocean.

Page 15

Student charts should include the following information:

- Rivers are fresh water; move along specific path unless they are flooding; used for drinking water and supporting wildlife; transportation. Rivers wear away land or deposit stone, gravel, and sand beyond their banks.

- Lakes are large pools of fresh water. Lakes do not move as rivers and streams do, though they may flood; used for transportation and recreation; support wildlife. They do not generally wear away the land like rivers and oceans do.

- Oceans are salty; they change the shape of their shorelines a little each day, either by adding to the land or eroding it away. Used for transportation, recreation; support wildlife

Page 17

Main Idea: Forests and wildlife depend on each other.

Summary: Forests help the environment because they prevent erosion, enrich the soil, and clean the air; they provide food and homes for wildlife. In return, animals scatter seed, bury nuts, and enrich the soil when they die and decay.

Page 18

Plants: grow long roots, store moisture in stems and leaves, grow thorns for protection from water seeking animals

Animals: burrow underground; stay away from the hot midday sun; come out only at night and in the early morning; get water from plants, seeds, other animals; store fat for times when food is scarce

Page 19

Answers will vary.

Page 20

I. A. They made their first homes from sod.

   B. They established farms and ranches.

II. A. Some prairie animals burrow underground.

   B. Some animals graze on tall prairie grasses.

Page 21

Report topics will vary.

Page 22

Entries will vary depending on the location.

Page 23

Poems will vary.

Page 33

Specific information will vary depending on the Native American group chosen.

Page 34

Fish: cod, halibut, herring, salmon (used for food)

Other Seafood: clams, crabs, mussels (used for food)

Mammals: seals, sea lions, otters, and porpoises (used for food, fur, and hides for clothing)

Page 36

Foods: berries, animals

Homes: cedar and other wood for long houses

Travel: wood for building canoes

Clothes: cedar bark

Tools: cedar bark for rope, mats, bows and arrows, fish hooks, storage chests, dishes

Totem Poles: wood for totem poles; ceremonial masks and rattles

Page 39

Hides: dresses, shirts, robes, shoes, tipis

Meat and fat: food; mixed with honey and nuts to make pemmican

Bones: needles and sled runners; other tools

The Native Americans became more efficient at buffalo hunting once they had horses.

Page 40

1. Hide is stretched or pegged to the ground.
2. Fat and flesh is scraped from the hide.
3. Hide is soaked with water.
4. Hair is scraped off.
5. Hide is restretched.
6. Hide is rubbed with sand and animal brains.
7. Hide is folded many times to soften it.

Page 44

Event: Totem pole raising

How Kwakiutl Celebrated: wore masks, heard speeches, sang, danced, and feasted

Event: Medicine dances

How Cheyenne Celebrated: raised tents to stand for mountains and a tree to represent the cycle of nature, heard myths, danced and feasted

Page 45

Answers will vary.

Page 46

North: women; **East:** door; **West:** guests; **South:** men

Page 47

Growing Corn: Changing Woman; **Weaving:** Spider Woman; **Sand Paintings:** Wind People

Page 54

1. They crossed the Atlantic Ocean to Plymouth to start a new colony.
2. Women and children stayed on the ship; men went ashore to hunt and dug holes in hills for shelter.
3. They learned how to grow American crops from Native Americans.
4. They learned from Native Americans.

Page 55

Answers will vary.

Page 56

1. There were no roads, only paths. The paths were too narrow for wagons. People had to cross the Appalachian mountains; some got lost.
2. Daniel Boone blazed a trail, his crew cut down the trees to make the road.
3. no bridges; lack of ways to repair broken wheels; attacks by Native Americans

Page 57

Answers will vary but should contain information from the reading as well as the students' own reasoning.

Page 60

Wilderness Road: from Virginia to Kentucky; no bridges, attacks by Native Americans, lack of materials for repairs, the Appalachian Mountains

Santa Fe Trail: from Independence, Missouri, to Santa Fe, New Mexico, and later, Los Angeles, California; dangerous rivers, high mountains; finding food and water difficult, especially in deserts

Oregon and California Trails: from Independence, Missouri, to Oregon; dangerous rivers, high mountains, snow-filled mountain passes

Page 61

February 12, 1809 Lincoln was born; **1858** Lincoln ran for senator; **1858** Lincoln debated Stephen Douglas; **1860** Lincoln became president; **1863** Lincoln freed the slaves in the South; **April 15, 1865** Lincoln died.

Page 64

Planes: Good: faster; **Bad:** expensive

Trucks: Good: goods are delivered right to the door; cheaper than planes and trains; **Bad:** slower than planes, smaller loads than trains

Trains: Good: can carry heavy products and large loads, cheaper than planes; **Bad:** can go only where there are tracks, cannot deliver right to the door; slower than planes

Ships: Good: can carry heavy loads, low cost; **Bad:** slow, can go only where there are waterways

Page 65

Products students find will vary.

Page 69

1. B; **2.** C; **3.** F; **4.** E; **5.** A; **6.** D

Page 70

Answers will vary depending on the president students choose.

Page 72

Plans will vary depending on the organization students choose.

Page 73

Reports will vary depending on the symbols students choose.

Page 75

Reports will vary depending on the states students choose.

FS-23223 Social Studies Made Simple ▪ © Frank Schaffer Publications, Inc.